PROGRESS
Can We Do Without It?

Massimo L. Salvadori

translated by
Patrick Camiller

Zed Books
LONDON & NEW YORK

Originally published in Italy by Donzelli Editore under the title
L'idea di progresso, copyright © 2006 Donzelli Editore

This English translation was first published in 2008 by
Zed Books Ltd, 7 Cynthia Street, London N1 9JF, UK,
and Room 400, 175 Fifth Avenue, New York, NY 10010, USA
www.zedbooks.co.uk

Designed and typeset in Goudy Old Style and Eurostile
by Long House Publishing Services, Cumbria, UK
Cover designed by Andrew Corbett
Printed in the EU by Biddles Ltd, King's Lynn
Norfolk

Distributed in the USA exclusively by Palgrave Macmillan,
a division of St Martin's Press, LLC,
175 Fifth Avenue, New York, NY 10010

A catalogue record for this book is available from the British Library
Library of Congress Cataloging-in-Publication Data is available

ISBN 978 1 84277 936 1 Hb
ISBN 978 1 84277 937 8 Pb

About the author
Massimo L. Salvadori is Professor of Political
Science at the University of Turin and one of
Italy's leading political thinkers. His previous
books include *Karl Kautsky and the Socialist Rev-
olution, 1880–1938*; *The Liberal History* and
Modern Socialism.

CONTENTS

To my grandchildren,
Elisa, Chiara and Tommaso,
and to all the little ones who
in their lives will have to face
unprecedented challenges.

Now that we have entered the twenty-first century, we find ourselves facing a major paradox. On the one hand, we live in a world that is changing at record pace, scoring ever greater triumphs in science and technology, and steadily effacing old boundaries in a sustained, majestic surge of development. On the other hand, confidence in the overall progress of humanity strikes us as a faith or illusion from another age. The great scientific-technological achievements and advances in social-economic development appear as so many gates beyond which the road is extremely uncertain. A growing number of people even fear that the road will lead to an irreversible decline in the conditions of human life. Their pessimism may turn out to be excessive and unfounded – but is in any event a significant and alarming sign of an unquestionably widespread contemporary malaise.

The idea of the continual progress of humanity as a solid possibility or even a necessary destiny has been overturned; it seems to have become either a fond hope or a myth from the past. Confidence in progress as an ongoing amelioration of spiritual-moral and material conditions – already a regulative ideal of human action in the eighteenth century, then a veritable and triumphal faith in the nineteenth – has been undermined by the spiritual and material evolution of humanity itself.

If we look at the fate of the idea of Progress in the old world that gave it birth, we may say that in the nineteenth century, acquiring the character and consistency of a new religious creed, it first penetrated the secular bourgeois elites. It then spread outward to the broad masses through the essential mediation of the socialist parties and reached an apogee in the twentieth-century communist movement. Finally, attacked and ridiculed by apologists for the regimes in power – nationalists and imperialists, anti-democrats, racists, anti-Enlightenment currents, anti-positivists and anti-socialists – it suffered a gradually deepening setback in two world wars. Its cause was not helped by unparalleled bloodbaths, cruel authoritarian and totalitarian regimes, genocidal ideologies and practices, serious deterioration of the remaining democracies, and massive use of science and technology to serve the violence of rulers.

After the nightmare of the Second World War, itself a reflection of all the failures of the previous era, a new phase – beset by new contradictions – got under way. A long period of strong economic growth took hold in the developed countries, democracy revived and consolidated itself in the West, and obsolete colonial empires collapsed and gave way to a series of new states. Yet, although economic development could increase the supply of material goods fairly consistently, and raise the standard of living for large sections of the working classes, many in the rich countries themselves were left in a precarious and marginal position, and too much of the rest of the world was prey to underdevelopment and extreme poverty. Meanwhile, the new superpowers held sway over a divided planet, gripped by a Cold War and overshadowed by nuclear terror. In these years the indiscriminate plunder of natural resources (of which people became increasingly aware only in the last few decades of the century) assumed the character of an unprecedented assault on the conditions permitting the reproduction of life. All these factors together added up to a sharp, and in many ways substantive, contrast to the vision of spiritual and material Progress that had first taken root in the West and then spread to the rest of the world. They clouded a shared cultural, political and social vista supposedly capable of opening the gates to 'universal regeneration'.

The refutations of Progress in the twentieth century were so overwhelming that we need to ask ourselves whether the chapter should be considered definitively closed. What has happened is that the progressive vision of harmonious functional growth – embracing science and technology, culture, the arts of politics and government, and the production and distribution of material goods – has disintegrated into its various components. Science and technology have developed in leaps and bounds, creating a truly indisputable credo that has spread ever more rapidly and pervasively throughout the world, whereas politics, government, production, culture and religion have undergone deep and often terrible fractures that have lacerated humanity or even torn it to pieces. With this decomposition of Progress as a single vector of improvement, the universal grammar of rapidly and ceaselessly advancing scientific-technological knowledge has been placed mainly at the service of political and economic forms liable to generate or reproduce deep splits within the human race. These splits are expressed in confrontational policies, in furious ideological wars and terrible armed conflicts, in economic strategies that have spawned development for some parts of the world and underdevelopment for others, and in the abnormal enrichment of certain strata in contrast to those with a modest degree of prosperity or the great majority who can barely, if at all, attain the subsistence minimum. The most telling sign of this process is that science, technology and economics have been largely confiscated by the power politics of certain states, by their ruling classes and opulent upper echelons. This is the dominant trend.

To be sure, the history of the twentieth century cannot be indiscriminately placed in the category of 'the negative'. As we have already mentioned, it produced along with the dominant trend a number of major advances: the fall of the totalitarian regimes, the end of the colonial empires, higher living standards for broad masses in the more developed countries, the affirmation and extension of new political and social rights, the march of women towards equality with men. Nevertheless, taking due account of the huge advances in some areas, a balance sheet at the beginning of the twenty-first century must still conclude that no country can look ahead with equanimity to its own future or that of others. There are too many outstanding problems and major question marks, which we may simply list here without trying to rank them in order of importance.

The first concerns the capacity to build institutions to handle the urgent global issues that extend as never before across the boundaries of existing states. The second refers to a model of economic development which, through its intensive application in huge countries such as China and India, has raised popular living standards to a degree never seen before, yet is based on an exploitation of resources so great that nature threatens to take potentially catastrophic 'reprisals' against humanity. The third is linked to the waves of migration that carry increasing numbers of poor and desperate people to the richer countries in search of new opportunities, together with an ethnic, cultural and religious diversity that creates rather complex and intractable problems of integration in the places where they settle.

The fourth concerns the impact of economic globalization, whether in severely undermining the welfare institutions that provided an effective safety net in the West for weaker sections of society, or in spreading job insecurity along with three decades of neoliberalism, or in creating a new model of development in many parts of Asia (especially) and Latin America. This is development that creates many jobs in previously excluded sectors, but also deepens imbalances inside the country and introduces often inhuman exploitation of broad masses who are ignorant of what their social rights are or might be.

The fifth has to do with the inexorable tendency to vast accumulation of wealth in the hands of small oligarchies, in a context where the gap is widening between the income share of the top strata and that of the middle or lower ranks of the social hierarchy. The sixth is bound up with the extension of democratic institutions in the world – a process profoundly eroded, however, by the declining capacity of those institutions to regulate economic and political oligarchies that dispose of enormous means to influence subaltern strata in support of their own interests.

The seventh is represented by the emergence of religious fundamentalisms, whose theocratic vision of political power and social relations challenges such achievements as the secular conception of the state, political and civil liberties, and cultural pluralism. The eighth may be traced to the idea that the acute conflicts of interest and the great cultural, political and social differences inevitably lead to a clash between two incompatible worlds of 'Good' and 'Evil', between which it is not possible to create any bridges. (Testimony to this idea are both Islamist terrorism and the ideology of Western neo-conservative forces geared to a global battle against 'rogue states' and a shifting realm of 'shadows'.)

Anyone who looks at these problems with open eyes, in

whichever way and whatever the gravity attached to them, cannot maintain the illusion of those in the nineteenth century who believed, with a variety of accents and hypotheses, that the forward march of Progress was assured. Indeed, the Progress of humanity has never looked as uncertain – one is tempted to say, unlikely – as it does in our time. But what way forward can there be if humanity gives up reflecting on what needs to be done, in a world threatened with nothing less than disaster? Perhaps such reflection will be assisted by an analysis of how the idea of Progress evolved: how it began as a guide allowing human beings to increase their range of ameliorative options, then mutated into a religious faith in a new providential order reliant upon objectively necessary mechanisms of historical development, and then finally became a fallen and discredited myth. In following this trajectory, we will be in a better position to ask whether, despite everything, we do not still need the idea – revitalized in a critical spirit, to be sure, stripped of its myth-like character and used, as it initially was in the Enlightenment, to identify possible ways of improving the human condition that should not be wasted precisely because they may also slip from our grasp. The Enlightenment thinkers who first elaborated the idea shared a fundamental optimism about the power of reason and the intellectual and moral virtues of Man. Two centuries later, we all have reasons to doubt that the future can be a good future. Yet we are alive and cannot cease trying to give the idea of Progress, however uncertain, a meaning and a value.

If, in this essay, I devote more attention to the vicissitudes of communism than to those of any other movement in our time, this is because of its extraordinary importance in the history of the twentieth century. On the one hand, it embodied the hopes that so many of the 'insulted and injured' had of a major improvement in the human condition or, better still, of final liberation from the terrible ills that had afflicted humanity in the past and continued to afflict it. On the other hand, although communism claimed to be not only the leading but the sole bearer of the idea of Progress, and to hold all the instruments needed to carry it into effect, its degenerate version of that idea turned its principles and values upside down. Instead it established a form of society based on political despotism, mental subjugation, spiritual conformism, and economic and social relations marked by the omnipotence of the totalitarian Party and state.

The short bibliography at the end of the book is intended to signal some key works for a deeper understanding of the argument, and to indicate the references that have been particularly important to the author.

1

THE PARABOLA OF AN IDEA

Inherent in the idea of Progress is a firm belief that it is given to humanity to pass from a qualitatively inferior to a qualitatively higher stage, in a sequence that will ensure a radically better spiritual and material life for not just a part but the whole of the human community. In this sense, it is a typically universalist idea. The means of progress, as variously defined by its champions, consist of an ever more practical use of reason, constant expansion of the sphere of rational activity, multiplication through work of the resources offered by nature, the development of more civilized customs, and the triumph of sociability over aggressive impulses up to the point of perpetual peace. Progress, therefore, means continuous and indefinite improvement of man's faculties and growing success in pursuit of the greatest possible individual and collective happiness, by means of a harmonious integration of rational enquiry, scientific research, technology, economic development, political and social institutions, and private and public ethics. Progress is destined to culminate in an order capable of preventing all the evils and crises that have previously marked the history of humanity. In short, the idea of progress includes the belief that a better future requires emancipation from obstacles left by the past which are blocking its way: old idols, prejudices, mentalities, customs and institutions grounded upon 'irrational' suppositions and traditions.

The idea of Progress, however, has been perceived in two ways that not only differ but decisively conflict with each other. In one perspective, it has been seen as a regulative ideal or aspirational model: a possibility always threatened by inadequacies and improper modes of thought and action. In the other perspective it is a necessary process, which has become intrinsic to nature and human development. Nature or society, therefore, may deviate only temporarily from the direction imposed by Progress as the necessary and objective course of history. The idea of Progress as a *possibility* found its main expression in European thought first among the seventeenth-century protagonists of the scientific revolution (who may be seen, with some reservations, as the proto-progressives) and then, above all, among the Enlightenment intellectuals and reformers of the eighteenth century; while the idea of Progress as an *objective necessity* is mainly identified with the nineteenth-century evolutionary positivists, whether liberal or socialist, and with the revolutionary Marxists. The former rested upon ethical, intellectual and practical commitment illuminated by a normative philosophy, and it had confidence in the subjectivity of political and moral choices; the latter gave to the social sciences, especially economics and sociology, the main responsibility for discovering the laws of historical necessity and providing accurate predictions about its course, so that action for political and social change could be scientifically oriented.

To explain the difference between the two conceptions, we may say that the vision of the seventeenth-century scientists and eighteenth-century philosophers always focused rigorously on both the presuppositions of Progress and the obstacles that might not only limit it but make it impossible to achieve. In their eyes the betterment of humanity could happen only through an option in favour of rationality and sociability, or through prudent use of scientific-technological instruments and the 'lights' of the mind, which should become man's principal resource under the permanent control of wise policies and morality. Nothing expresses the meaning of all this as well as the metaphor of the flame, which, though intended to give light, could always go out and restore the empire of shadow. The idea of Progress peculiar to Enlightenment thinkers, the true originators of the idea as such, emerged against the historical background of modernity's flood tide: the great voyages of discovery, the expanded limits of the physical and cultural world, the growing international-ization of trade, the choice of tolerance as a reaction against ideological repression and civil and religious wars, the discoveries of modern science and their technical applications, the circulation of ideas beyond national boundaries and the formation of a cultured and gradually more cosmopolitan public opinion, the modernization of state institutions, the rise of a liberal or absolutist reform-ism and, at the end of the parabola, the crisis of the *anciens régimes*. Progress, then, appears to have thrived on a wider knowledge of the world, the exploration and increased understanding of nature, an awareness of the relativity of values, struggle against fanaticism, a quest for means of promoting civil co-existence, a conviction that peaceful trade could prevail over violent acts of war and conquest, and an interchange between cultures as well as their growing internationalization. This all came down to the conviction that a new ethic and enlightened legisla-tion could remove the obstacles placed by 'the old world' in the way of mutual improvement.

For the Enlightenment thinkers, then, Progress repre-sented an idea and a force to be asserted through thought and action, with the potential to become a reality through the appropriate mobilization of energies and resources and the momentum gained from an ever-broader consensus. This approach is especially evident and sure-footed in Voltaire and Diderot, so attached to the benefits of reason but also so alert to the dangers that threatened to extinguish its light. It was only right at the end of the parabola of Enlightenment culture that Progress as a possibility and a regulative ideal of practical action gave way to the idea of a movement guaranteed by historical necessity. This latter vision had already manifested itself in the late eighteenth century, though in a conceptual context not without unresolved ambiguities; in his later work Condorcet maintained that history should be seen in terms of a succession of stages, and that it would reach completion in the final emancipation of forces capable of securing Progress against any negative power that might have held it up. In essence, the Enlightenment conception claimed to bear witness to three kinds of perfectibility: the perfectibility of the individual's rational and ethical faculties; the perfectibility of enlightenment itself, originating as the patrimony of elites but coming to be shared by ever greater numbers of people; and the perfectibility expressed in the tendency of humanity to become more united, thanks to its sharing of a single universal reason.

Although the positivists inherited the characteristic Enlightenment belief in human potential for progress, they sharply diverged from it in their identification of what we might call the engine of Progress. The Enlightenment thinkers were children of a pre-industrial society, whereas the nineteenth-century positivists grew to maturity in an expanding industrial society; the former appealed to the reason of intellectuals to show the way and to policies of reform to travel it, whereas the latter made the social sciences responsible for getting political elites to understand that they should not block the objective laws in the machinery of development but should clear away the obstacles that the past had strewn in its path. The Enlightenment thinkers feared that the light might be extinguished; positivists and evolutionists such as Saint-Simon, Comte and Spencer no longer saw Progress in terms of confidence in the power of good values or the possibilities that a shared reason offered to individuals and communities, but established a scientistic-religious faith in the objective forces of history, which, by virtue of necessary laws of development, had reached a stage where Progress itself had the character of an irresistible immanent law. At the heart of the positivist idea of progress was the nineteenth-century process of industrial modernization. This suggested that the union of the social sciences with scientific research, industrial technology and institutional engineering had given birth to a combined power capable of carrying humanity forward from a state of submission to nature and history to an age in which it would extract untold riches from nature, multiply them by overcoming any limit ever imagined and distribute them in the most bountiful of ways. Hence too the conviction – here is the qualitative leap from the Enlightenment's conception of Progress as problematic – that it was now possible to plan the future scientifically, and that it was up to social scientists to point the way forward for the rulers of society. It was the ultimately 'positive' age of technology and industry, where the social and natural sciences were unified in a single science whose components were connected to one another organically and practically; the mind was thus able to discover and render operational the objective laws of reality.

History ceased to be a succession of unconscious men and women ruled by the rise-and-fall cycles of an obscure Providence; it could acquire the nature of a plan,

consciously drawn up by social scientists and realizable
under their guidance in a way that would lead to constant
improvement. Ethics, politics, economics: everything
should become scientific. And science meant a capacity
for prediction and planning. Saint-Simon was loud in his
praise of technocratism, Comte of organicism and sociocracy, and Spencer of biologism. Darwin's scientific work
and his theory of natural evolution were eventually taken
over by the followers of positivism as the paradigm for a
theory of progress in which society inevitably passed from
a lower to a higher stage. The necessary march of progress
would one day guarantee the arrival of peace on earth:
between the scientific elites (the priestly caste of the new
religion) and the masses, between different states and con-
tinents. It was also a common belief that wars and
religious, political or social conflicts would be made futile
by the progress of industry and commerce, by the increase
of wealth, and by the sovereignty of science in all spiritual
and material activity. Comte, the founder of sociology,
transformed the positivist philosophy of progress into a
liturgy, a religion of humanity, a scientistic church with its
own hierarchies, symbols, rituals, saints and places of
worship.

Although the positivists shared certain assumptions,
they divided quite profoundly over how to understand the
ideological, political and social foundations of this
inevitable progress. On one side were the bourgeois
liberals, who conceived progress and the order that should
result from it within a framework of market mechanisms
and individualism; on the other side were the 'organi-
cists', with the evolutionary socialists as their historically
most important current, geared to the collectivist organization of society. But all these displayed the same enthusi-
asm and the same faith in the invincible power of science,
technology and industry, seeing it as the basis for an

explosion of resources that would satisfy constantly new needs in ways never imagined before and, by extending development out from Europe to the rest of the world, unify the whole of humanity. This brought to a climax the Enlightenment idea of indefinite improvement entrusted to man's rational and moral faculties, and of a politics guided by them. However, it also altered that idea by postulating the myth of the primacy of infinite material progress, in which industry dictated the roads to be taken by knowledge, morality and politics and thereby transformed the history of the human race from one of spiritual and material poverty, limitation and suffering to one of growing prosperity based on firm social cohesion. The old pessimistic realism – political in the case of Hobbes, economic and social in that of Malthus – was now obliterated. One exception among the economists and political philosophers of the nineteenth century was John Stuart Mill, who, though a firm believer in the improvement of humanity, was far from accepting the promises and slogans of those who claimed that progress was guaranteed.

The communism of Marx and Engels, and the international socialist movement associated with their ideas and teachings, fully shared the belief in the historical necessity and unstoppability of progress; one might even say that they belonged in its front ranks, having placed themselves in important respects on the road first opened by positivism. The explicit link to positivism was stronger and more evident in Engels than it was in Marx, whose revolutionary philosophy and analytic categories showed the crucial influence of Hegelianism and its dialectical system, although he interpreted it in such a way as to replace the idealist matrix with a materialist formulation. Moreover, both Marx and Engels were severe critics of the positivists' technocratism, organicism and biologism and of their

tendency to create a new scientistic religion. Yet the link
to the positivist idea of progress appears very solid, since
their communism was based on faith in the infinite perfectibility of the human race made possible by the powers
of science, technology and industrialism and by the
spreading of development from its European heartlands
to the backward peripheries. They also shared with positivism in particular a conviction that science was now
capable of dictating its own laws for the governance of
both human beings and material things. Not by chance
did Marxism define itself as 'scientific' socialism and take
on board a view of the world based on historical necessity.
At the same time, however, the conceptual grammar of
Marxism, its analytic structure and its theory of the
dynamics of political and economic development were in
crucial respects quite different from, and even opposed to,
those of positivism. For, although it too believed in historical necessity and objective laws of human development,
and although, like Comtean doctrine, it envisaged a succession of stages rising from lower to higher degrees of
complexity and maturity, Marxism saw the key to historical advance not in gradual evolution from one stage to the
next but in the revolutionary dialectic, the class struggle
and the breakdown of the capitalist system. These would
be the driving force of the great transformation destined
to carry humanity from 'prehistory' to a new history
culminating in universal peace, harmony and self-
government, under the guidance of science and economic
planning – a history in which the recurrent danger of a
war of all against all would finally give way to a general
benevolence of all towards all.

Marxism identified a particular social stratum, the
modern proletariat, as the historical agent which, thanks
to a revolutionary palingenesis, would overcome the trau-
matic structural crisis of the bourgeois-capitalist system

and achieve the unification of the human race, guided –
in an elitist touch typical of the Enlightenment and
positivism – by a conscious minority of communists in
possession of revolutionary wisdom. In the end, therefore,
the Marxist vision of how history would take shape – an
end to class struggles and differences, to conflicts between
rich and poor, rulers and ruled, property-owners and
propertyless, town and country, intellectual and manual
labour, developed and undeveloped countries – formed
part of the complex adventure expressed in the Enlightenment idea and the positivist conception of progress,
however much it differed from these in relation to the
society of the future and the grand reorganization that
would lead to it. We might even say that Marxism was the
most radical manifestation of that complex adventure. It
should be added that not only Engels but also Marx
ended up flanking the Hegelian dialectical component of
his thought with far from secondary elements of a
Darwinian naturalistic evolutionism; and that the theoretical influence of positivism made itself deeply felt in successive generations of Marxists, many of whom blithely
combined positivism and Marxism and in reality gave the
former precedence over the latter.

Whatever the prevailing theoretical matrix, between
the final decades of the nineteenth century and the early
years of the twentieth, socialists became the most fervent
champions of a (variously conceived and pursued) idea of
Progress. This should be related to the fact that, in the
ranks of the bourgeoisie, the number of believers in
Progress was sharply declining – owing to fears of socialist
revolution, the growth of imperialist and racist creeds, an
aversion to the democratization process because it was
seen as raising the faceless masses above the social and
cultural elites. Many intellectuals of diverse persuasions,
of whom Nietzsche, Spengler and Sorel may serve as

examples, came forward to flay the whole idea of progress: the first openly disparaged the Christian egalitarian ethic, socialism and democracy; the second spoke in prophetic tones of the end of the cycle of Western civilization and the approach of Caesarist rule; and the third denounced the 'illusions of progress' cultivated by bourgeois liberals and gradualist currents within the workers' movement.

Only socialists continued to believe in the possibility of dissolving the old world and founding a new one that would bring the boons of civil and international peace and prosperity for all individuals and all countries. It should be borne in mind – especially in view of later developments – that, although nineteenth-century socialist revolutionaries believed that violence would be necessary to secure the transition from capitalism to socialism, they mainly understood it in the social sense of expropriating the expropriators and bringing the means of production under the ownership of the workers' state, in a context where active resistance on the part of a handful of 'reactionaries' might need to be temporarily put down. In any event, physical repression would be contained, since the goodness of the socialist project and the iniquity of the old aristocratic-bourgeois order and capitalist exploitation would ensure an overwhelming consensus in favour of the great transition. The objective maturity of socialism, resulting from the necessary laws of history, meant that in the transitional period political conflict among the subjects of society would be reduced to a marginal phenomenon. We see the strength and preva-lence of the evolutionary schema in their thinking.

In the first half of the twentieth century, however, the ideas of Progress formulated both by the Enlightenment and by nineteenth-century positivism and socialism were thrown into complete confusion. While disenchanted realists of various persuasions denounced it as an illusion outside time and history, those who stood under the banner of communism offered themselves as the leading defenders of Progress, indeed its only true inheritors, but reconceptualized it in total opposition to the theories of social democracy. In communism, the idea of libertarian progress assumed a millenarian character: it became a political religion with its own clergy and elites, who controlled the mass of believers spiritually and organizationally within a rigidly hierarchical framework that realized, in unforeseen ways, certain aspects of the old Comtean project. The common denominator linking this to the tradition of the eighteenth and nineteenth centuries was the goal of indefinite improvement of humanity; the discontinuity was a dramatic rejection of any schema involving peaceful evolution, and a conviction that the means to a new world should rely not on ethical and rational universalism (now only a final objective after the great unification of humanity) or on a gradually increasing attractiveness of the project, but rather on the violent overthrow of power relations and existing institutions, and on an epochal civil war between social classes, political formations and competing world-views. At first, twentieth-century communism also nurtured illusions that a rapid transition from the old to the new society could restrict political and physical violence to a passing secondary role, but it soon took on a more clearly defined character and painted violence in quite different colours. Thus, apart from fairly small minorities of the progressive liberal-democratic bourgeoisie, the only forces in Europe that remained wedded at this time to an evolutionary, gradualist and peaceful conception of progress were the reformist currents of social democracy. A rising tide of wars, political and social conflicts and deadly, hate-filled ideological clashes opposed millenarian revolutionaries not only to reactionaries, imperialists, right-wing anti-democrats and racists, but also to liberal democrats and reformist socialists, with the result that both on the left and the right a new momentum was given to supporters of hierarchical power relations dominated by pure force, and to a straightforward 'friend–enemy' dialectic with no room for anything in between.

In the first half of the twentieth century, then, hopes that the conditions would be created for peaceful, evolutionary change were irrevocably dashed as a result of imperialist conflicts, two major world wars, the advent of Bolshevism and fascism, the horrors of Nazism and its genocidal climax, bloody wars associated with colonial oppression, economic and social crises that sowed poverty and a sense of insecurity, acute social and political confrontations, atomic extermination tried out on Japanese cities, and a torrent of hate – ethnic, racial, religious and cultural. Cosmopolitanism, universalist internationalism and pacifism collapsed in the face of wild outbreaks of particularism. States, nations, classes and races (the latter concept, though based on unscientific prejudice, was still operational and largely taken for granted) armed themselves against one another in savage homicidal conflicts which frustrated and derided the feeling, even more than the concept, of belonging to a common human species and the idea of rational guidance as a virtue and benefit for all. Among communists, the goal of infinite perfectibility – which not only failed to disappear but actually became a founding matrix and ultimate objective – generated some perverse manifestations as it underwent a radical change in meaning and function.

The striving for a new epoch, a new history, a new society was stronger than ever on both the left and the right. But it took the form of an 'assault on heaven' – an exalted projection of millenarian dreams on the part of subjects such as the state, the nation, the class or the race in whose name it was thought possible and necessary to trample with impunity on individual and collective rights. The assault on heaven no longer relied on the spread of universal reason and the unifying benefits of social-economic development, cultural dialogue and internationalism, but indiscriminately asserted the superior 'reasons' of the relevant state, nation, class, party or race. The spirit of these absolutist particularisms manifested itself in various kinds of parochial shrillness, through the unlimited use of force against enemies up to and including the extermination of hundreds of millions of people. All this found its extreme expression in totalitarian visions of the future, in which any manipulation or violence was permitted against societies and peoples, and an extraordinary degree of power was joined to the modernization process and the idea that parts of humanity had a 'mission' to dominate and even crush others. The trajectory of communism unfolded fully within this framework, its originally universalist ideals and projects distorted and swallowed up by the methods it used in practice. Eventually all that remained was the poisoned well of an abstract neo-millenarianism divorced from reality, which became more and more discredited until its epilogue of self-destruction.

To conclude: the original founding nucleus of the eighteenth and nineteenth-century idea of Progress – that is, the unity of spiritual and material improvement – has split apart and disintegrated; the unitary conception has given way to one of progress in discrete areas: science, technology, the economy, and so on. These advances, let us be clear, have been hugely important and produced awesome results. But too often they have benefited particular countries, particular social strata and political or economic minorities, mostly serving not to achieve greater unity but, on the contrary, to widen existing gulfs and to sharpen the opposition between different components of humanity.

In quite unforeseen ways, the course of history threw into crisis one of the cornerstones in the thinking of all currents that associated themselves with Progress. While they theorized and pinned their hopes on harmonious development of the spiritual and material foundations of human existence, these currents did not hesitate to treat the natural world as a source to be used without limits. Nor did they have an inkling of the problem that might arise from the relations between *homo faber* and mother earth. The vision of science, technology and industry in previous centuries reflected what we might call a state of unconscious innocence with regard to human manipulation of the natural environment. The bosom of nature appeared immensely fruitful and bountiful. Its exploitation did not seem to pose any problems other than that of organizing the necessary instruments ever more intensively and efficiently. The diffuse optimism that marked the nineteenth century and much of the twentieth was a clear sign of this defective vision. The industrial revolution and its sequel, the dizzying advances of science and technology, had ceaselessly fuelled and justified it. But the ever more intensive exploitation of natural resources, pursued in a spirit of endless feasting and considered a totally irrevocable and irrefutable success, gradually acquired the character of frantic violence against nature, which now emerged as a new danger to accompany the violence that humans inflicted on one another. Thus, if the first half of the twentieth century threw Progress into deep crisis as a result of wars and political and social violence, the closing decades carried the crisis into the realm of man's relations with the environment, so that nature started acquiring the features of an offended stepmother in revolt against her abusers.

The idea of Progress, born out of enormous confidence in the human destiny, described a parabola in which we can see how much that confidence has been shaken. It was a manifestation of the firm, almost indestructible, belief that humanity was capable of leaving behind for ever the uncertainties of its past and entering an era of great security. Now, however, we are pervaded by a growing sense of insecurity, as the suspicion gradually dawns on us that humanity is on the point of losing control of the helm as it heads towards grave dangers of its own making.

2

REFORMISTS AND
REVOLUTIONARIES

If we turn now to the forces in the early twentieth century that claimed to have inherited the idea of Progress from the two preceding centuries, it is easy to see that they were mostly affiliated with the cause of international socialism. The components were of the most varied hues, for the socialist movement was made up of many socialisms. Each one bore the imprint left by a number of factors: national, cultural and in some cases ethnic differences; distinctive levels of economic and social development; activity either in liberal parliamentary states under the hegemony of the capitalist bourgeoisie, or in military-bureaucratic empires with semi-liberal or decidedly autocratic institutions; a particular relationship between revolutionary and reformist currents; either a strong party organization which, enjoying the support of trade unions, was able to exert a decisive influence on the working classes, or else conditions of isolation sometimes not rising above the level of a sect. All these socialisms, whatever their specificities, had a common foundation in their faith in Progress. They believed in a future of universal peace, equality, material prosperity and a higher cultural level for all.

As socialism sank deep into the consciousness of broad masses, the idea of Progress underwent extensive and momentous changes. It ceased to be the property of a minority of intellectuals and politicians who, feeling especially able to understand the path indicated by the light of reason, offered their various recipes for the future of humanity. (This had been true of the Enlightenment elites, of the socialist thinkers who drafted bold programmes of reforms and models of a new society, and of the positivist 'social scientists' who analysed historical development and thought they had discovered its laws.) From the time when the socialist parties, and the masses organized by or favourably disposed to them, embraced the idea of Progress, it ceased to be an intellectual reading of the world and lost its originally aristocratic character: it became, to use Saint-Simon's formulation, a 'new Christianity'. For, among the socialist masses, it was already widely believed that the Christian churches had set themselves up as conservative bulwarks of the socially privileged classes, and that socialism was the true continuator of Christ's original message of universal equality and fraternity which had been betrayed by the earthly powers and their priests.

The socialists promised the 'coming of the kingdom' that early Christians had vainly awaited as the prelude to the celestial world. In socialism, the idea of Progress rested on a mixture of science and faith. Belief in a coming kingdom of equality claimed to base itself on a science of social development, whose laws had established that the fall of the evil capitalist order and the triumph of first socialism and then communism were historical necessities that no subjective force would be capable of resisting. The great theorists of this 'scientific' socialism, such masters as Kautsky and Plekhanov following in the footsteps of Marx and Engels, did not allow any objections on this score; their convictions, translated into a popular register, became the creed of millions and millions of workers and activists, who saw them as prophets of the age ahead and guarantors of the truth of the message of rebirth. In the period spanning the nineteenth and twentieth centuries, 'scientific socialism' witnessed the uninterrupted growth of the international workers' movement and became the dominant ideology within it.

Nevertheless, there seemed to be a parallel with the history of Christianity, which, after waiting in vain for an early end to the old society and the coming of the new kingdom, had struck previously unthinkable compromises with reality and inserted itself into the institutions regulating human relations. Similarly, once it had become clear that capitalism, despite periodic crises, retained its strength in the economically developed countries – while the path to revolution looked ever less assured – the socialist movement was impelled to adapt to the unexpected situation that had slammed a firm brake on the impatience of its followers. The solution that prevailed was a split between theory and practice. The great majority of socialists remained convinced that the revolution would come about one day through the collapse of the capitalist system. But since, in countries that had political and civil rights and representative institutions, the working classes increasingly obtained the right to vote and modest gains in living conditions, the socialist parties and associated trade unions took the road of possible progress on an ever larger scale, inserting themselves into the existing institutions and fighting for reforms (even if they accepted them only 'with reservations', as a 'partial settlement' in comparison with what would be achieved on the day of the revolution).

In short, the socialist parties and trade unions gradually integrated into 'the system'. The basic trend was clearly visible, albeit with significant differences, in Germany, France, the Austro-Hungarian empire, Italy and elsewhere in Europe. The only major exception in this respect was Britain, where the labour movement, only marginally penetrated by Marxism, had always had an openly reformist, gradualist conception of its role and had never embraced the myth of total regeneration through revolution.

Such was the state of European socialism in the final years of the nineteenth century and the opening years of the twentieth, when Eduard Bernstein, formerly an orthodox Marxist, subjected Marx's theory to a revision that was in reality a frontal critique. Deeply influenced by Britain's experience of an advanced capitalism and mature liberalism, and by the sensitivity of its ruling class to the requirements of political and social reform, he argued in effect that Marxism was no longer able to explain the modern economy. This led him to put forward the following theses: (1) it was illusory to await the collapse of capitalism; (2) the emancipation of the working masses would come not from the revolutionary doctrines of an obsolete ideology but along the path of reforms; (3) parliamentary democracy should be thought of not as a liberal disguise for the dictatorship of the bourgeoisie, but as a conquest that allowed freedom and creative action for the workers too – which the socialist parties should utilize, defend and help to consolidate; (4) the socialist parties, in seeking to enlarge the frontiers of democracy and reforms, should abandon the sterile notion of a wall between the proletariat and all other classes and learn to establish suitable alliances with progressive liberal-democratic forces; (5) socialism was faced with a capitalism capable of renewing and therefore sustaining itself, and so the socialist goal of ever greater social equality should be seen not as a historical necessity but as a possibility to be made reality through competition with capitalism in the framework of parliamentary-democratic institutions.

When Bernstein advanced these theoretical positions, together with a gradualist and reformist programmatic strategy, the main response of the international socialist movement was outright rejection. Bernstein's revision of Marx's theory was regarded by his critics as an unacceptable yielding or capitulation to bourgeois liberalism, or even as an act of betrayal. The defenders of 'orthodoxy' – Kautsky and Rosa Luxemburg in Germany, Plekhanov and Lenin in Russia, Antonio Labriola in Italy, to mention only a few emblematic names – branded him as a renegade. Yet the split between revolutionary theory and reformist practice, already widely operational in the Western socialist movement, had the effect of largely isolating theoretical revisionism without preventing a *de facto* reformism from sinking deeper and deeper roots.

The 'possible socialism' to which Bernstein looked as the way forward rested on several presuppositions: an enlargement and consolidation of parliamentary institutions and the liberal matrix of political democracy; a strengthening of the workers' movement through an alliance, where suitable, between socialist parties and liberal-progressive currents representing the middle strata; and the introduction of reforms, backed up by a growing popular consensus, to achieve a more equal distribution of cultural and material resources in a climate of internal and international peace.

The revolutionary theorists, who had some well-honed weapons at their disposal, argued that Bernstein's evolutionary optimism failed to take into account the growth of authoritarian tendencies among the aristocratic-bourgeois ruling classes in response to the sharpening of class struggles, as well as the fact that the great powers were increasingly inclined to resort to imperialist wars to settle their conflicts of interest. In their view, the marriage of authoritarianism and imperialism was leading inevitably to world socialist revolution. The concept of Progress held by the revisionist reformists, according to which socialism was a historical possibility rather than a necessity, gave new topicality to the Enlightenment idea of the light of reason as a flame which evil human actions could extinguish and only constant effort could keep burning or reignite. The revolutionary position, by contrast, drew on post-Enlightenment scientism and its underlying faith in unshakable historical necessity and the objective laws that governed it.

Events between the two world wars spectacularly refuted in Europe both the optimistic expectations of the gradualist reformists and the ideological triumphalism of the revolutionaries. Instead of the development of liberty, democracy, social reform and peace, the dominant trends were authoritarianism, totalitarianism, militarism, imperialism, total war and the dialectic of revolution and counter-revolution. But these did not lead to the collapse of capitalism, the irresistible rise of the working classes, the victory of world socialist revolution, and a transitional dictatorship against the old classes nevertheless based on proletarian democracy. Rather, there came a succession of economic and social crises and political convulsions, a frenzied wave of imperialism, continued isolation of the Russian revolution and its rapid descent into a new despotism, and finally the defeat of socialists and communists by hostile forces in all the major countries of Western and Central Europe.

In this context, the division of the European and international workers' movement culminated in a bitter confrontation between socialists and communists. Although both currents never stopped calling for unity of the working class, they became implacable enemies once their positions in relation to the First World War and the communist revolution in Russia placed them in opposing and rival camps. A number of socialist tendencies and parties positioned themselves in the middle, drawing closer now to one, now to the other of the two main poles. This split, never to be overcome, grew deeper in the interwar and postwar periods as social democrats lined up against Soviet totalitarianism on the side of reformism and parliamentary institutions, while the communists took opposite positions. So great was the antithesis that the two components of the workers' movement were unable to build a degree of unity adequate to their common interest in confronting the fascist threat to Europe; the repeated efforts in this direction proved to be weak, temporary and ultimately ineffectual.

The large composite formation which has been defined, in contrast to communism, as 'social democracy' first came into being in the period from the beginning of the twentieth century to the First World War, and acquired its definitive shape in the years between the Russian revolution and the late 1940s. As is well known, before the split in the European workers' movement between reformist socialists and revolutionary communists and socialists, the term 'social democratic' was simply synonymous with 'socialist', and many workers' parties adopted it. Even the Bolsheviks, for example, were members of the Russian Social Democratic Labour Party until in 1912 they effectively constituted themselves as an independent party and in 1918 formally gave birth to the All-Russian Communist Party. Events linked to the outbreak of war in 1914 and later to the Bolshevik revolution crystallized the elements that would finally shape up against each other in 1918–19 as social democracy and communism.

The objective roots of social democracy in this sense of the term were laid in Western and Central Europe in the twenty years preceding the First World War, through the integration of the socialist parties and associated trade unions into the state-political and economic system – a process which induced or, we might even say, increasingly compelled them to restrict the revolutionary goal to the level of ideology and to pursue reformist strategies and methods in their practical activity. Subjectively, however, this process was experienced in three different ways. First, revisionists of the Bernstein school wagered on reforms as both a means and an end, with the aim of giving the state and economy a more and more social character. Second, those who were called 'centrists' because of their intermediate position between the revisionists and revolutionaries generally remained faithful to Marxist theory and rejected the revisionist critique, but in practice followed the path of reforms and gradualism and were attacked by radical socialists for having a merely passive revolutionary ideology. Third, the consistently revolutionary groups, present as a minority in each socialist party, maintained that capitalism was nearing its end, that even positive reforms could not affect its system of exploitation, that economic development was dominated by great capitalist oligarchies, and that these were pushing countries toward inter-imperialist wars which would fan class conflict and lead to socialist revolution. In the eyes of these groups, the revisionists were disarming the revolutionary proletariat theoretically and the centrists were disarming it practically. Ideological radicalism and the revolutionary spirit, which in Germany found their worthiest expression in Rosa Luxemburg, were carried to their extreme point by the Bolsheviks under Lenin's leadership in the Tsarist empire. The development of the above three tendencies, and their clashes with one another during the period before the First World War, may be seen most clearly in the largest European socialist party, the German SPD, then considered the centre of international socialism.

To understand the differences that were shaping up in

the European socialist movement, it is necessary to relate them not only to declared ideological positions but also, and above all, to the conditions of life in the various countries of the continent, that is, to working conditions and wage levels, social legislation, possibilities of political participation, development of representative democratic institutions, psychology and attitudes among the working masses and their organizing cadre in the parties, trade unions and parliaments. In the economically most advanced countries, whose institutions, despite the persistence of considerable blockages, had been undergoing significant democratization, the still quite widespread appeal to the catalytic function of proletarian revolutionary violence was becoming less clearly defined within the socialist parties. A desire for job stability was tending to predominate, together with an appreciation of, and determination to defend and enlarge, political rights or social gains. Socialist society was conceived more and more as the result of consent, obtained at elections among the working masses once they had become a majority of the sovereign people. To be sure, in continental Europe, unlike in Britain where the labour movement was firmly wedded to reformism, this process was unfolding in anything but a linear manner. In no country could democracy be thought of as truly consolidated: its limits and elements of fragility, the policies and periodic threats of the most authoritarian ruling-class groups, sometimes encouraged a rekindling of radical tendencies to the detriment of the reformists. This was clearly visible in Italy, for example. Yet the reformist mole kept tunnelling below ground, primarily in the trade unions.

A quite different evolution was taking place in the Tsarist empire, where an autocratic regime combined complete arbitrariness with a system of privileges for the upper classes. Here, notwithstanding the reform of 1861, the broad mass of the peasantry continued to live in a state of serfdom and extreme poverty, while the new mass of factory workers thrown up by industrialization was paid starvation wages and deprived of political and trade-union rights, and much of the intelligentsia consisted of rootless individuals frustrated in their ambitions. There was open and uninterrupted warfare between the regime and the ruling classes, on the one hand, and the revolutionaries on the other. It had been declared after the failure of the peaceful 'going to the people' movement in the late 1870s, when so many of the middle-class and upper-class youth who took part in it had had their idealistic illusions shattered by the refusal of the peasants to welcome them as educators. This had created favourable conditions for the formation of terrorist groups, who paid with their lives or with deportation for attempting to 'execute' leading figures in the tyranny: high officials, governors, generals, even the Tsar. Recourse to violence in its most crude and direct forms then became part of the faith for all Russian revolutionaries.

But, in the early years of the twentieth century, whereas supporters of the Socialist-Revolutionary Party continued to uphold acts of individual terrorism, the Marxists wagered on the violence of the proletarian class and armed revolution to destroy the Tsarist order. The fact is that anyone looking for a better life in Russia could see nothing other than obstacles to be torn down. The country had no tradition of political and civil liberty with which it could link up, no previous experience of democracy. From the late-seventeenth to the early-twentieth century, the dialectic of preservation and inno-vation had worked itself out entirely within the country's small leading group; modernization processes had always and only come from the top down. The regime offered no hope, then, and any hope there was seemed to lie in the use of force to dismantle everything and start building again. This was the situation in Russia at the beginning of a century that would witness three Russian revolutions. No wonder that, within the Russian socialist movement, reformism had no echo and no real practical significance outside a few intellectual currents.

The great majority of socialists in the Tsarist empire were intransigent revolutionaries. This was true of the descendants of populism, organized in the Socialist-Revolutionary Party, who dreamed of a national socialism that would give expression to the collectivist traditions of the peasant *mir*; and it was also true of the Marxists, who, after the foundation of the Russian Social Democratic Labour Party in 1898, foresaw the development of modern capitalism in Russia as the objective precondition for a revolution of the proletarian masses. When Russian social democracy divided in 1903 between the Mensheviks led by Martov and the Bolsheviks led by Lenin, the issue in dispute was not at all whether a violent revolution was the only way to overthrow the Tsarist regime. But there was a deep split over how the revolution should be understood and carried out, and what its goals and perspectives were. The Mensheviks looked to the West and foresaw that, while they were waiting for conditions to ripen for socialism, Russia would become a modern capitalist country in which the liberal bourgeoisie assumed state power, that an era of parliamentarism, political democracy and freedom for working-class organization would ensue, and that all this would have the civilizing effect that had always been lacking in Russia. For the Mensheviks, the course led first to the overthrow of Tsarism and then, once the necessary economic and social conditions were present, to socialism. The main protagonists would be the working masses, ever more developed and conscious of their interests and objectives, under the leadership of a

Marxist party that rejected terrorism and was open both to internal pluralism and to a contest among competing currents.

The Bolsheviks had a quite different, indeed opposite, approach. Their leader, Lenin, in keeping with the canons of Marxism, also believed that Russia would have to pass through a stage of capitalist development before it could arrive at the socialist revolution, but unlike the Mensheviks he thought that nothing positive could be expected of the feeble Russian bourgeoisie, since it lacked the necessary strength and resolve to overthrow Tsarism and create a parliamentary-democratic republic. Consequently, the end of the Tsar would see the working masses give birth to a 'democratic dictatorship' politically guided by social democracy and other revolutionary parties, whose aim would be to promote capitalist development under their control. This democratic dictatorship would make way for the 'dictatorship of the proletariat' once the more advanced countries of the West had ushered in the impending era of socialist revolutions already inscribed in history; this would initiate the world-wide upheaval foreseen by Marx.

For our purposes in this book, however, the most interesting aspect is not Lenin's ideas regarding the economic and political development of Russia, but the ideology expressed in Bolshevism. As we have seen, others were arguing for a revision of Marx's doctrine, on the grounds that it was outdated and unable to account for the new reality of capitalism, that it was tied to violent methods and the dictatorship of the proletariat as the means of achieving socialism, and that it was deaf to the liberal legacy of political and civil freedoms and the need to pursue reforms by forging alliances with middle strata open to the requirements of progress. Lenin's answer was that Marx's doctrine was omnipotent because correct: he

denied any validity or legitimacy to revisionism, scornful-
ly dismissing it as a Trojan horse in the camp of international socialism and forcefully criticizing those who
verbally defended Marxism but sided in practice with the
revisionist reformists. Any doubt concerning Marx's
thought was culpable and unacceptable; its omnipotence
came from the fact that it allowed those who kept faith
and followed it to control the course of history. The Bolsheviks thus took to considering themselves Marx's only
true disciples in Russia (and later in the whole world).
But, while proclaiming their orthodoxy, they actually
practised a special kind of revisionism by bending
Marxism to their requirements in the particular conditions of Russia.

The Mensheviks, more faithful to Marx in assigning to
capitalist economic development the task of creating a
strong, educated and mature working class within the
Russian empire, insisted that the class struggle between
capital and labour, together with the political struggle
between parties in a democratic republic, would steer the
working class towards socialism on the basis of its own
experiences, and that the Party would gather the fruits of
this process in giving it a political direction and a strategic
outlet. The Bolsheviks, in the spirit and style of a Russian
tradition of neo-Jacobinism, countered this with a very
different line based on a demiurgic conception of the
Party as the only possible repository of socialist consciousness. In this view, the working masses, not to speak of the
wretched mass of the peasantry, did not incline spontaneously toward the revolutionary struggle for socialism,
but tended to submit to the baneful influences of the
established order, to defend their own sectoral interests,
and to obtain illusory partial improvements without going
beyond a perspective of immediate demands. It thus
became deeply rooted in the Bolshevik psyche that they

were the true guardians of the faith, an elect minority called upon to keep watch against the Tsarist enemy, but also against all other class enemies: weak and inconsistent Marxists, revisionists who brought division into the ranks of the revolutionary army, and backward sections of the masses who were sensitive, or even enslaved, to the influence of their adversaries. They had no doubt that they held a monopoly of the truth.

It was on this conception and this psychology that Lenin developed his theory of the party between 1902 and 1904. It divided the body of society between genuine champions of progress and their enemies, and socialists between true and false socialists; the tried and tested socialists, the Bolsheviks, had the task of steering history towards its inevitable revolutionary goal, which nothing and nobody could stop. Bolshevism thus introduced one of the extreme forms of the friend–enemy dialectic into the body of the Russian socialist labour movement. It was necessary to build the Party in accordance with a rigid top-down schema: the leaders at the top were the keepers of the science of revolution; the middle cadre consisted of people trained by the leadership to execute its directives; and the rank-and-file were called upon to spread among the working masses the line formulated at the top and passed down by the cadres. All were expected to devote their whole life to the revolution, choosing it as a 'profession' from which there could be no turning back until the goal was reached.

The Bolsheviks thus gave birth to their own millenarianism, in an unsentimental and prophetic form typical of religious sects of the past but inspired by the purity of revolutionary science. The truth of which they felt themselves to be the main bearers was deposited not in the Jewish-Christian Bible but in the texts of Marx and Engels – finished scriptures of the science of society that explained the evolution and laws of its previous history, governed present history and would govern the process of anti-capitalist revolution up to the advent of socialism and communism. The wretchedness of human life in the Tsarist empire, a closed, self-protective system of power permeated with social, political and police-style violence, had taught them what the terrorists of the previous generation had learned before them: that the sword of the oppressors had to be opposed with one that was even sharper and more resolute. But they had also learned from Tsarism – whose spirit, as Rosa Luxemburg soon understood, had profoundly influenced them – the further important lesson that the role of the masses before their socialist liberation and regeneration was to obey orders from the top.

The Russian privileged classes, perpetuating in the empire a characteristic attitude of Europe's *anciens régimes*, thought of peasants and workers as beasts of burden to be held down and used as supports for their own material prosperity; the Bolsheviks, who sincerely looked ahead to the emancipation of those masses, considered them in the present context of massive economic and intellectual backwardness as material to be moulded and bent to their own purposes. The Menshevik idea that the working masses should be the subject of the revolution was considered by the Bolsheviks as neither more nor less than an ideological prejudice, an expression first and foremost of analytical rather than political weakness. The role of the masses was to constitute a hammer in the hands of professional revolutionaries, who alone knew how to use it and against whom it should be directed. The signs of an authoritarian conception of power in this line of thought and action were immediately evident in the polemics that broke out within Russian social democracy, as well as outside it, at the moment of the split between Mensheviks and Bolsheviks. After that, there were always those who accused the Bolsheviks of holding a neo-Jacobin conception of power and showing an unacceptable lack of confidence in a working class that they placed under a deadening tutelage; it seemed a road to the dictatorship of a minority, or even of a single man – a road to the degeneration of socialism. The Bolsheviks responded harshly to such criticism and in effect proclaimed themselves to be new Jacobins: they held the true Marxist science in their possession; they were supporters of a super-centralized Party organization; they were needed to guide workers who had been blinded by the corrupting influence of the hostile old world; and the Mensheviks were pseudo-revolutionaries in the thrall of a doctrinaire sentimentalism. The split between the two wings of the party would never be repaired.

We need to ask why it was the Bolsheviks, not the Mensheviks, who prevailed and eventually won the day in Russia. The first determinant was the direction in which the Tsarist empire evolved between 1903, the year of the split in the party, and 1917, the year when Lenin and his followers triumphed. For the Menshevik line to be successful, history would have had to take a different course: a victory for bourgeois-liberal forces in the 1905 revolution; the founding of a solid parliamentary-democratic republic in a framework of cultural and party-political pluralism; the rapid development and 'civilizing' of Russian capitalism as a whole; the rise of a vigorous class of small and medium-sized landowning peasants in the countryside; the conquest of trade-union and organizational rights by factory-workers; the ability of socialist parties to compete freely in defence of their own ideas and later, when conditions were ripe, to put themselves forward as candidates for the exercise of power; and a sufficiently long period of institutional stability both inside the country and externally. This was the scenario on which Menshevism had pinned its hopes. But in reality history developed in quite a different way, eventually burying Menshevism along with Tsarism and bringing Bolshevism, within fifteen years of its birth, to establish a regime even more absolute than the Tsar's that would fulfil the 'prophecy' of Lenin's opponents.

Having become, in the end, the enemy of all other forces – aristocratic, bourgeois, counter-revolutionary, liberal, Menshevik, Socialist-Revolutionary, anarchist – Bolshevism certainly did overthrow the old world, but at the same time it displayed its legacy to the full in the dictatorship of an ever more restrictive minority exerting an iron grip on the whole of society, until it repressed and abolished all political and civil liberty and all cultural freedom, and annihilated any individual, group or class held guilty of opposing the sole legitimate bearers of Progress. Such Progress could not be challenged because it was necessary, because the forces putting it into practice had absolute knowledge of the 'laws of history' and, not by chance, had gained total victory over their multiple enemies. In the minds of the Bolsheviks, Progress was the child of an ideology developed by an omniscient political elite – an ideology which, once the new age dawned, would give way to the advent and rule of 'universal reason' in the form moulded by that elite.

If we look at how the situation in Russia developed between 1905 and 1917, we see clearly which set of factors prepared the way for the defeat of Tsarism, then of liberalism, the Socialist-Revolutionary Party, Menshevism and anarchism. It was a period that tended to inflame relations among the various social groups and classes, fanning hatreds at the extremes and seeming to give a mathematical demonstration that the path of reforms was blocked, illusory, ineffectual. Tsarism gave full proof of its obstinacy in defending an outworn system, and the messages it gave to the people were nothing short of disastrous. 'Bloody Sunday' and the repression in Moscow during the 1905 revolution, the granting of a pseudo-parliamentary system that remained in place from 1906 to 1914, the failure of the agrarian reforms devised by Stolypin (who met opposition from the big landowners, before falling to a terrorist pistol in 1911), the massacres that were the regime's response in 1912–13 to mass working-class and peasant agitation, Russia's participation in the First World War without the necessary preparations and the resulting sacrifice of millions of poorly armed, inhumanely treated men on the altar of Tsarist dreams of imperial power, the spread of corruption, the mass hunger among poor strata of the population – all these factors helped to widen the gulf between those who aimed to hang on to fratricidal power at any cost and those who had been confirmed in the belief that no compromise was possible.

Rather than in 1917 – a year in which the illusion took wing that the transition from the old to the new regime could take place with a fairly limited degree of force – the final showdown between reactionaries and revolutionaries was acted out in the terrible civil war that followed, when it seemed clear that victory would go to the side capable of exercising violence with the greatest success. The value of individual life, traditionally rather low in Russia, sank closer to zero. Reactionaries and Bolshevik revolutionaries found themselves joined together in a common disposition and psychology: for the former it was a question of saving Russia and its 'venerable' institutions, for the latter one of rising to a 'new' humanity and a 'new' society. But both were prepared to climb over heaps of corpses to carry out their 'mission'.

This disposition to violence, which totally dominated life in Russia after the outbreak of the world war, developed unchecked in Western Europe too, where the conviction took hold that it was the only way to cut the knot of irreconcilable interests both within the body of society and in relations among states. Ideologies support- ing no-holds-barred struggle as a means to resolve political and social conflict gained enormously in strength during the First World War. In the eyes of growing forces on both the right and the left, liberal democracy was so discredit- ed that it seemed like a mere relic close to extinction. In the belligerent countries, the mass of soldiers were reduced to cannon fodder, the crudest *Realpolitik* inspired every aspect of the terrible conflict, expansion of its own power was the goal of each state, and the political, bureau- cratic and military elites increasingly held the view that the broad masses were merely a vast terrain for manoeu- vres. These were the factors fuelling a tendency to violence among militarists, nationalists and reactionaries as well as among left-wing radicals. The message everywhere seemed to be that hobnail boots were the winning card, that the world was irreversibly divided into the strong and the weak, and that it was up to the strong to impose them- selves by crushing the weak; the calls for a dictatorship became more and more vigorous.

In such a context, the new demiurges could see no sense in the idea of possible Progress through the march of civilization, based on gradual reforms, the shared exercise of reason and certain fundamental moral values, and respect for political and civil pluralism and represen- tative institutions. As the values and principles of democracy, liberal pluralism and reformism grew steadily weaker, the conviction grew stronger that the sceptre of politics belonged to those who were prepared for bold and decisive action. This category of people mainly divided into reactionaries and revolutionaries: the former turned to the myth of a restoration of order and hierarchy in new forms against red subversion, worthless democracy and decadent liberalism, while the latter backed the myth of a complete overthrow of the bases of established society, a radical demolition of capitalism, moribund aristocracies and bankrupt institutions of the bourgeoisie. For the revolutionaries, Progress had become irresistible because history was preparing an epochal change that no subjective force would be capable of halting. It was up to the revolutionaries to further, by their own conscious action, the coming of the new world inscribed in the iron laws of history.

The Great War had the effect of tearing Russia apart and accentuating to the extreme its internal political and social conflicts. The fall of Tsarism in February 1917 triggered a phase of merciless struggle among the various currents competing for power, and in October the way was opened for the Bolsheviks, led by the revolutionary genius of Lenin, to take the reins of government; they could rely on a superior level of organization and solid armed nuclei, their hand strengthened by the collapse of the old institutions and a social-economic catastrophe that was radicalizing soldiers, workers and peasants *en masse*. With the coming to power of Bolshevism, communism began its journey from the ideal sphere to reality, first in Russia, then in a large part of the rest of the world.

Those who begin to reflect on the twentieth-century vicissitudes of communism have to take on board a number of hugely significant historical facts. First of all, in a century that saw the rise and fall of many other movements of exceptional importance, communism occupied a unique position in the sense that it made a global political and social agenda revolve around itself. Its genesis as an active political force in Russia at the beginning of the century, then its victory over Tsarism and its creation of a new type of state linked to an International with worldwide ramifications, then the formation of a corona of states, including the immense China, into a 'socialist camp' opposed to the capitalist camp – all this gave it the appearance of a phenomenon that literally dominated its epoch. For nothing happened without taking it into account. Its overpowering ascent justifies comparison with the dynamic that led Islam to transform itself, in a brief space of time, from a tiny religious sect into a gigantic political and military empire.

Second, communism confronts us with the undeniable fact that a force whose goal was to combat every form of oppression, to engender a society of equals, to end the domination of privileged minorities over the masses, of rulers over ruled, to educate society to self-government and to promote it in practice – that this force led to the creation of one of the most oppressive forms of social and political organization in history, to rigid new privileges that opposed the few holding absolute power to everyone else, to institutions based on permanent violence, and to terroristic practices of oppression and extermination on a vast scale. Hence the question of how to understand the relationship between the 'utopia' – which played a key role in recruiting successive waves of people, numbering millions all around the world, into the ranks of the communist parties – and an outcome that was such a complete negation that communism ended up bankrupt both as an ideal and as a political and social system. Once a realization of this reached the summits of power, communism went down in a sudden implosion that has no precedent in modern history. The question of how this happened is all the more important for two reasons: on the one hand, the ideal negated by the practical results was for many communists not an instrumental ideology but a living faith, for which huge numbers sacrificed themselves and even gave their lives; but, on the other hand, when those same communists became aware of the reality – here we leave aside all those, especially in the capitalist countries, who were victims of the illusions fuelled by their national parties and the Soviet and other communist regimes, and who never knew what communism in power was really like – they not only continued to support the cause of a degenerate regime but unhesitatingly defended it with all manner of mystifications.

So, how was it possible that a political ideology and practice whose ambition was to turn Progress 'from utopia into science' was finally buried beneath a pile of material and spiritual rubble? How, in this process, was the original doctrine interwoven with the subjective intentions and actual historical events that transformed communism into an ideology and a practice of oppressive power? Was it adverse historical conditions which caused the perversion, or overturning, of the original ideology, or was the gnawing worm already present at the beginning?

3

COMMUNISM IN POWER

Communism acquired the form that made it one of the dominant forces in the twentieth century in the years between 1914 and 1921. Before then, although the Bolsheviks had a specific identity and effectively operated as an independent party, they were still a radical component of Russian social democracy and the Second International. The break with social democracy became final with the crisis in the International brought on by divisions over the war, the effects it was likely to have, the tasks it imposed on European socialist parties, and the general relationship with the crisis of capitalism and revolution. In 1914 the International remained largely passive at the moment when peace was under threat, and once war broke out the socialist parties in every West and Central European country – with the opposition of a minority – voted in their national parliaments in favour of war credits and gave their support to their respective governments. In Russia, when a majority of Mensheviks fell in line with the nationalist wave, evoking the threat posed by German militarism, the foundations were laid for an ever deeper split. Communism now took shape through denunciations of the 'betrayal' by Western socialist parties, which had supposedly capitulated to imperialism by supporting a war that reflected the contradictions leading to the imminent collapse of capitalism. In this view, bourgeois democracy had demonstrated its bankruptcy and a whole civilization had turned into its opposite; the only possible response to this was not a return to the *status quo ante* but world socialist revolution.

In the years of the great European catastrophe, communism had two major components: a western one in Germany and an eastern one in Russia. The first was routed in the years immediately following the war, but the second came to power through the October Revolution in 1917 and, having managed to consolidate itself, placed itself at the head of an international communist movement. It had its main German exponents in Rosa Luxemburg and Karl Liebknecht, and its main Russian exponent in Vladimir Ilyich Lenin, supported by Lev Davidovich Trotsky. They all shared the conviction that the socialism of the Second International had suffered an irreversible defeat, that revolution was the right response to the crisis of the old order, that the proletarian parties fighting for a new society had to be given a political leadership and organization which measured up to the task, that the time had come to break with and fight head-on the socialists discredited by support for their imperialist governments.

Despite this common denominator, however, there were not only divergences but highly significant disagreements between the leaders of German and Russian communism, with implications for the whole conception of the revolutionary process based on assessments of the human factor. As humanists, Luxemburg and Liebknecht saw revolution as the liberation of all human beings from the twofold degradation of oppressing and being oppressed; it would be the work, above all, of the toiling masses of Western Europe, who had been trained for participation by decades of political and trade-union struggles, who were inspired by the ideals of equality and civil rights, and who were convinced that any recourse to proletarian violence was justified only as a temporary response to the hostile action of other classes. Nothing was more alien to them than the dictatorship of a party acting as tutor and master of society and itself subordinate to a narrow circle of leaders, in the belief that the working class was organically inferior from a political point of view.

In this respect, they were close to the Mensheviks and as distant as one could imagine from the Bolsheviks. Whether or not their utopia was achievable, it was the powerful and sincere nucleus of their conception. Not by chance did Luxemburg bitterly criticize Lenin's theory of the party in 1904, denouncing it as a neo-Jacobin deviation, an expression of bourgeois-style authoritarianism, a justification for ruthless centralism and the committee rule of conspirators who felt omnipotent and were prepared to build a throne for themselves in the name of an emasculated popular will: in short, a reversal and restoration of Russian absolutism. In 1918 Luxemburg renewed her critique in even more energetic terms, directing it this time not only against Lenin's theory of the party but against the work of the Bolsheviks in government. And now the target was no longer just Lenin but also Trotsky – the man who in 1904, in the most radical tone, had joined her in the fight against Bolshevism, but in 1917–18 had become its number two. The Bolshevik dictatorship, she argued, meant the suppression of all freedom: it was suffocating the living roots of society, generating new privileges, spreading the seeds of spiritual and political corruption, making use of a demoralizing terror, choking the liberty of socialists along with that of non-socialists, making any democratic life impossible and rendering democracy meaningless for the proletarian masses themselves.

By contrast, Rosa Luxemburg's radical-democratic utopianism was based on the idea that a communist regime could draw its legitimacy solely from the support of the toiling masses, as the majority of the people. Socialism should not and could not be decreed by a minority, in a situation that was enormously immature both culturally and socially; the use of terror to crush the enemy was a sign of material strength but also of political weakness. It was certainly to the credit of the Bolsheviks that they had reignited the flame of revolution, but their organic defect was to guard it with forms of power that contradicted the values and objectives of socialism.

The attitude of the Bolsheviks, whose struggle to capture and consolidate power found its main exponents in Lenin and Trotsky, was therefore quite different from, and in some respects totally opposed to, Rosa Luxemburg's and Karl Liebknecht's conception of communism. Both during and after their lifetime, the two Russian leaders were described by many of their firmest adversaries (in Lenin's case from the beginning, in Trotsky's after his conversion to Bolshevism) as political geniuses but also power-hungry individuals, contemptuous of any humanity other than themselves and their followers, inveterate Machiavellians comparable even to Hitler and his acolytes, who used the demiurgic power of their personalities to launch a successful assault on heaven – but an assault that ended with a descent into hell.

This is a one-sided and simplistic interpretation. So too is the thesis that the two leaders of Bolshevism – with intentions that were 'pure', in the sense of Lenin's project of an egalitarian, self-managed society finally rid of bureaucratism and police or army apparatuses, which he advanced in 1917 before the October Revolution – eventually had to bow to the force of highly unfavourable circumstances: the isolation of the Russian revolution following the failure of the international revolution, for which the social democratic traitors were largely to blame; the pitiless civil war, which made it necessary for the Bolsheviks to have a monopoly of power in their hands; and the weight of Russia's backwardness on the shoulders of the new Herculean forces, who, in order to defend the trenches and use them to relaunch a general attack on the old world, made the survival of the Soviet state their highest *raison d'être* and paid a price they would never have wished to pay.

Now, the Bolsheviks like Rosa Luxemburg did believe sincerely in a new world: they conceived of it as infinitely better than the one they had overthrown in Russia and aimed to overthrow everywhere else. They believed in the unification of the human species, in an end to all exploitation of man by man, in the right of all to have access to common resources to improve their lot. And they looked ahead to an age of harmony without oppressors, without conflicts in society or between states, where the state itself would tend to disappear into a universal brotherhood and swords would have been melted down and turned into ploughshares. Nothing entitles us to think that the Bolsheviks did not pursue these goals with genuine conviction. Nevertheless, the means that Lenin and his followers developed to reach their objective (means at first rejected but later enthusiastically adopted by Trotsky) were vitiated from the beginning, so to speak, by a combination of elements.

A Machiavellian realism was fuelled by scientistic dogmatism, in the typical spirit of religious sects certain that they have been singled out for a mission to regenerate the world, so that their own orthodoxy has to be imposed at any cost on the corrupt run of humanity that cannot see for itself what is true and good and needs to be illuminated. Hence, the true believers were not at all inclined to await the birth of the new out of the clash of diversity, out of a consensus achieved by means of democracy and pluralism. In their view, the new world could arise only if an elite of professional revolutionaries came to power and purged society of its infected parts, wielding class violence in the hands of scientifically trained believers. The fact is that, although the Bolsheviks sought to overturn the spiritual and material backwardness of Tsarist Russia, they remained culturally and intellectually in its thrall – unlike the Mensheviks, who for that very reason were eventually 'eradicated', in a line of continuity which, in all too many respects, linked the old and the superficially new Russia.

The Bolsheviks – in keeping with the canons of socialist tradition – certainly would have preferred to achieve their goal without recourse to terror and physical violence (at least on such a vast scale), and to have promoted the broadest participation of the working masses. But, as the facts clearly demonstrate, they were prepared to renounce this option at once if obstacles appeared in its path, and to remove such obstacles with all available means in order to draw closer to the happy shores of the future world. All that counted was the future state of humanity, not the fate of individuals in the here and now. In this sense, as Rosa Luxemburg clearly saw, the Bolsheviks fully inherited the 'spiritual' legacy of absolutism and did not hesitate to give it a further twist. For, although the Tsarist autocracy had placed society under police surveillance, building gallows, filling prisons and deporting oppositionists to Siberia, the scale and harshness with which it had done this bore no comparison to the merciless repression conducted by its successors in power. Indeed, when the Bolshevik leaders had been arrested and deported, they had endured material conditions and restrictions on their freedom that seem 'liberal' beside the methods they used when they came to power.

The trajectory of the Bolsheviks in power is highly illuminating. In order to understand it, we must fully grasp how they saw themselves as the pure embodiment of the idea of Progress and the only force entrusted with its realization. Since Progress was inevitable and necessary, their task as its agents was to remove any obstacle in its path. However, when we analyse the positions of Lenin in particular, the problem of a glaring discrepancy has to be faced: that is, the gulf between his idea of a new 'libertarian' revolutionary state, which he propounded before October, and the one-party dictatorship, exercised over opponents and working masses alike, that ensued. It relied on a total centralization of power, a merciless apparatus of police repression, and the use of state terrorism to crush declared and supposed enemies and to control society by reducing the much-hailed proletarian democracy to an ideological myth unrelated to the real world. This discrepancy, which represents a radical counterposition, was assumed by the 'justificationist' Lenin and Trotsky to be irrefutable proof that the party dictatorship corresponded to a state of emergency brought on by unfavourable historical circumstances, and not at all to the values and goals of Lenin and his followers, who always intended to implement the utopia once the old history had ceased to impose itself on the new. An indubitable gulf remains, however, between Lenin's vision of a proletarian state marching towards its own extinction and giving way to the self-government of society, and the Soviet dictatorship based on an extreme, despotic intensification of the powers of the state. Hidden within this gulf is an aspect which has to be explained if we are to understand how the utopian project and the realities of power rested upon a revealing common denominator: namely, both the state supposedly withering away and the state continually strengthened in its power rested upon a monolithic conception that applied to the whole revolutionary process.

On the eve of the seizure of power, when Lenin wrote his famous pamphlet on the relationship between state and revolution, he intended it as an essay in Marxist theory valid for all countries that history summoned to the great transformation. His premise was that the collapse of the old world would have a decisive impact: on the one hand, it would rapidly put to flight the enemy classes and their institutions and remove their possibilities of resistance; on the other hand, it would make it possible to build the basic structure of socialism on an international scale. There would be a smooth road to the construction of the new society and to a spontaneous popular consensus behind the revolutionary socialists and the rapid self-organization of the working masses. It has been thought rather 'strange' that the theorist of a party of professional revolutionaries, who had intransigently argued that the masses tended spontaneously not to revolution but to defence of their own economic interests, suddenly began to praise the spontaneous action of the masses and no longer said a word about the party, so rigidly exalted in the past and destined to be the fulcrum of Bolshevik power in the future. However, this line of interpretation does not take one key aspect into account: Lenin grounded his theory of the party-demiurge on the link between the negative spontaneous tendencies of the masses and the corrupting influence exerted on them by capitalism and bourgeois or pseudo-socialist reformism. So, if the party-demiurge does not feature in the essay on state and revolution, and if the spontaneity of the masses is held up as eminently creative, this is because Lenin thought that the revolutionary process then under way had finally created favourable conditions for the old corrupting influences to be swept away, that the Marxist word had finally become flesh, and that the virtues of the masses, illuminated by an awareness of the unstoppable advent of socialist society, would now be able to make themselves apparent.

Lenin took it for granted that Russia's backwardness would be swallowed up in the now certain world revolution. In a context where the old world and the classes linked to it were collapsing, democracy could have meaning only as democracy of the proletarian masses, that is, a society in whose ambit the party would no longer need to fulfil its function of guidance and education as a centralized elite in opposition to hostile political forces capable of 'bending' the spontaneity of the masses in a negative direction. But the revolution was victorious only in Russia, and the roots of the old world, instead of being swiftly and definitively torn up, exerted a powerful grip on the country and the new regime. When it became clear that the October Revolution remained isolated, the Bolsheviks continued to hope for a time that the world revolutionary process had simply paused. But then they had to face up to the reality of their solitude – to economic disaster, appalling poverty, sharp political and social conflicts, civil war, and implacable international hostility. And so, until better times dawned in the future, Lenin's utopian vision on the eve of the October Revolution was indefinitely consigned to the celestial heights of ideology.

Between October 1917 and the early 1920s, the Bolshevik leaders gave a highly significant response to history's non-fulfilment of their deluded hopes. Precisely because they were sure of being the subjective force that could unlock the gate to the road of Progress, they thought it their mission to retain power at any cost and in the face of any difficulty. They succeeded in crushing all their enemies and internal oppositionists: from the white generals to representatives of the old classes, from the socialist revolutionaries and Mensheviks to the anarchists, from the hostile peasantry to workers who became restive when they were left without bread. After dissolving the Constituent Assembly, they put an end to all political pluralism, slapped strict controls on cultural life and laid siege to the Orthodox Church. The doctrine of the super-centralized party, which Lenin had developed between 1902 and 1904, became the definitive foundation of one-party rule. The 'Jesuits of the revolution' and their handmaiden state became absolute masters of society, while the police forces in charge of repression acted as their armed wing.

A phase of even greater centralization accompanied the clampdown in 1921, when the Party suppressed all pluralism in its midst to confront the wave of working-class agitation and peasant opposition, the insurrection of the Kronstadt sailors (once more guilty of untrustworthy spontaneity), and the concessions it had been forced to make in its New Economic Policy to small and medium-sized traders and businessmen, so as to revive an economy on the brink of collapse after the catastrophic experiment of 'war communism'. The official watchword, 'All power to the Soviets of workers, soldiers and peasants', became in effect: all power to the top of the Party. The supreme task was to hold out until the mirage of international revolution, in which they continued to believe despite the disappointments, turned into a reality. The forces of God's new chosen people had to be mobilized under the steely guidance of its priests, to cross the desert and reach the Promised Land on the day when the workers of the world would break their chains and join the Bolshevik heroes. This was the doctrine of the Bolshevik revolutionaries until the dying Lenin left the helm of the Party and state. As fate would have it, the last hope that Germany would join its forces to those of Bolshevik Russia was dashed in the extremist and amateurish attempt at revolution there in October 1923, a few months before Lenin's death in January 1924.

How did the Bolshevik balance sheet look in 1924? The world revolution had not taken place, but the communist regime in Russia had quite unexpectedly managed to survive and consolidate itself, while around it the parties grouped in the Third International had been growing stronger. Despite the failure of the world revolution, then, communism had become a major factor in international politics. Lenin's utopian vision of a proletarian state tending towards self-government by the masses had never got off the drawing board – on the contrary, the foundations had been laid for the first form of the modern totalitarian state ruled by the top leadership of a single party. This reversal of utopia that reality had brought about led the communists to come up with diverse and even opposing answers. There were some who, no longer having much or any sympathy for a utopian project that had no chance of being realized, set themselves the 'realistic' task of strengthening communist rule and the Soviet state in a bitterly hostile international environment, and of launching a process of economic modernization to further that end. Their main exponent was Stalin, the man whom Lenin, shortly before his death, had asked to be removed from positions of power because of his brutality and lack of loyalty.

But there were others – a minority – who looked with concern at the negative effects of the monolithic bureaucratization of power (though they too had helped to build it), and who concluded that the regime would totally degenerate if there were not an international revolution (though none was on the horizon) and a second proletarian revolution in Russia against Stalinist rule. They therefore moved into opposition, among the ranks of the 'heretics' and the persecuted minorities. The champion of all these forces was Trotsky, who in the past had triumphed alongside Lenin. There were also groups of Western communists, mostly consisting of intellectuals and political leaders of minority currents – men such as Karl Korsch, Arthur Rosenberg, Anton Pannekoek, Victor Serge and Amadeo Bordiga – who from their various positions agreed that Bolshevism, both in the Leninist 'Vulgate' and in its Stalinist and Trotskyist forms, had gone off the rails of Marxism; these were the 'ultra-heretics' of communism.

In the end it was the mass of ordinary believers who, in their unshakeable faith, regarded Soviet Russia as a beacon that nothing could extinguish. Their yearning for a world of equality was impelled by the sufferings of the past and present, by the mountain of injustices, and by the fact that without a solid human and political anchor their identity would fall apart. The absolute need for a utopia made them blind and deaf to the reality of communist Russia. For these victims of Soviet propaganda, the totalitarian Bolshevik regime was the steel which had passed and would pass every test and challenge, and which, when the conditions were favourable, would finally lead to the realization of utopia. Convinced that the 'difficulties' in the way of Soviet socialism were all attributable to negative 'external' influences, they believed that the totalitarian regime itself was laying the basis for future self-government through the creation of a unified society, and through the application of Marxism-Leninism by an infallible party.

The totalitarian spirit thus became the new foundation for a faith in unstoppable Progress, which could be achieved so long as one was prepared to accept any price in political and social violence. Generations of communists internalized this doctrine, seeing the horrors of totalitarianism – when they saw them at all – as due to obstacles inherent in the 'transitional' era and the necessity of dictatorship. In Russia, the ranks of these believers consisted of Party members and cadres, senior technicians, bureaucrats and managers, who looked to the regime to pull the country out of its backward condition, to construct the bulwark of world communism, and to pave the way for the egalitarian millennium. In the capitalist countries, they consisted of sections of the working masses and intellectuals who, feeling deep human concern in a historical period of recurrent crises, blamed capitalism and its ruling classes for all the evils of exploitation, unemployment, poverty, oppression, political and social conflict and international wars, and projected their hopes of a better life on to a Bolshevik Russia, where the world of the future was gestating before spreading, sooner or later, to the rest of the earth. Their fortress was psychologically and emotionally closed, intellectually impenetrable to any doubts sown by the enemy: whether by capitalist and bourgeois elements seeking to destroy and discredit the Bolshevik regime, by social democratic defenders of fraudulent bourgeois democracy, reformist saboteurs of the proletarian revolution, or fascists and reactionaries who were sworn enemies of Bolshevism and its emancipatory potential. Any arrow aimed by such foes at Soviet reality was poisoned and mendacious – and therefore inadmissible.

In the course of a few years, from 1923 to 1929, the Soviet regime resolved its internal ambiguities. Lenin died early in 1924, prey to the keenest anxieties about the future of the state he had created. But the scenario had completely changed by the end of the decade. Stalin then held all the levers of the Party and state in his hands: he had defeated his opponents within the Bolshevik leadership, given the Party a unified ideology under the banner of Marxism-Leninism, with himself as its sole interpreter, branded as heretics and enemies of the people all those communists and non-communists who contradicted him, 'Stalinized' the parties of the Third International, and mobilized the violence of the repressive apparatuses against the peasant masses and other social strata who stood in the way of a complete state monopoly of economic life and the supreme goal of modernization and greatly increased military strength. For the group of leaders around Stalin, the utopian vision of a state withering away in a context of proletarian democracy, popular self-government and an end to class privilege had lost all meaning. They did not repudiate the utopia itself, because that would have meant a devastating loss of ideological legitimacy; indeed, they exalted it more than ever before, only within an empyrean sphere of petrified values where it had the role of a sacred but lifeless icon. It was like the process that affected the Christian utopia after it had lost its initial explosive momentum, at once acclaimed and totally negated by a hierarchical church bent on acquiring and preserving earthly power and the wealth of its ruling elite.

Stalin ruled the Soviet Union unchallenged for a little more than twenty years, from the end of the 1920s until his death in 1953. Never, in theory, did the idea of Progress achieve such a triumph as in that country and that period; but its humanist foundation – the rights of individuals and society and their emancipation from oppressive forms of power – was thoroughly negated in practice. Stalin achieved the synthesis of these opposites by promoting Progress to the official ideology of the state – a state which presented itself as the means to the greatest possible improvement of the human condition, but which in doing so assumed the right and the duty to crush with terror any enemy of the Party, any obstacle that individuals, groups or classes placed in the way of the noblest goal that had ever existed: the construction of socialism, and then of communism. In this synthesis, the dictatorship appeared as a regime which sought to clear the way for Progress by bringing the whole of society under its vigilant totalitarian control; it claimed to derive its legitimacy from the struggle against all forces opposed to Progress, and from the need to render these harmless by means of systematic spiritual and physical repression. The other side of the coin was constant mobilization of the faithful against the enemies of Progress, in an attitude of servile conformity to the thought and action of the single party, its leaders and, above all, its supreme leader. All opponents were reduced to non-persons without a voice and without any rights. The Soviet idea of Progress thus acquired the features of a society subject to the totalitarian power of a small minority.

It became the firm conviction of millions that the New World guided by the communists was turning Progress from an idea-force and myth into a tangible reality. During the Stalin period this conviction sank deep roots, overcame all doubts and repulsed all criticism; it even survived his death for some twenty years, until it started to become gradually clearer, on an ever wider scale even among believers, that communism in power was not leading to the goal supposedly determined by the necessary laws of history. For a long time, though, belief in this historical necessity was shared not only by simple people and devout Party militants but also by intellectuals, many of great stature, refined culture and sophisticated intelligence, who turned themselves into enthusiastic propagandists for the conquests of socialism. A whole series of victories were read as irrefutable confirmation that true Progress had ceased to be a hope 'without a place' and found assured domicile in the Soviet Union.

The first such victory was the success of industrial modernization in the 1930s, the second was the defeat of

Nazi Germany, and the third was the 'extension of the frontier of socialism' – which put an end to Soviet isolation and established a whole 'socialist world' – and the consolidation of a ring of communist parties in the capitalist countries that were linked to Russia by a dual thread. Stalin was literally idolized, as an earthly god possessing supreme powers of both body and mind, while the system of communist rule was considered the incarnation of the one true Reason. The light of political and social science, monopolized by the leaders of Marxism-Leninism-Stalinism as the source of universal enlightenment, replaced the light of reason that the thinkers of the Enlightenment had seen as the patrimony of the educated and, potentially, of anyone who acquired the conditions for its proper use. The idea of Progress was thus absorbed into a typically pyramidal system of command, run by a 'priestly' caste with a singular pope-like figure at the top. The frontier between the champions of Progress and its enemies (those who propagated obsolete traditions, prejudices, false beliefs and impostures) became the line between supporters and enemies of the New World.

Stalinism completed the perversion of the idea of Progress into a doctrine of the totalitarian state. The final chapter of this process came in the Brezhnev era in the 1970s, when the totalitarian regime reduced ideological dissent and political opposition to a mental illness to be 'cured' in psychiatric hospitals as well as internment camps. For, if the socialist state was self-evidently the embodiment of Progress, and if the Party was the indisputable guide on its march to ever greater perfection, then what else could opposition be but a phenomenon of diseased minds unable to stop themselves acting in a criminal manner?

4

NAZISM AND THE MYTH OF LOST PURITY

Enlightenment, positivism and Marxism, however different from one another, conceived of the improvement of society as a struggle against negative legacies of the past and therefore as a forward march that humanity had to follow into the future.

In the European crisis following the end of the First World War, the longing for salvation through a great change found one of its major expressions in communism. The other was represented by National Socialism. After taking shape in the early postwar years, it went on to an explosive victory in Germany in the 1930s and used all the instruments of power to launch its millenarian revolt; the aim was to change the face of the world in accordance with the designs that Hitler – who assumed in his person the role played by Lenin and Stalin in Russian communism – had formulated and announced in the previous decade. The two movements had a number of important features in common. Both grew and came to power in a country already plunged into a devastating internal crisis. Both declared war on what they saw as an old system of life and values, preaching the necessity of its violent destruction and the birth of a new world. Both proclaimed that they were the only force capable of purifying and pacifying society and stabilizing a new order. Both therefore maintained that only the dictatorship of their party could safeguard and develop the conquests which had been achieved mainly through their resolute action. Both deployed a system of repression against all their opponents and had systematic and permanent recourse to terror.

Nevertheless, the theory of salvation had opposite cultural and ideological presuppositions in the two movements. Whereas for communism the improvement of society required closing the door on the past and marching forward to create a new kind of civilization and humanity, for the Nazis it was necessary to turn back and recover the original roots of the only authentic possible civilization, which had been distorted and now ran the risk of being totally lost if they were not sought out, recognized, restructured and revitalized. Communism was a universalist ideology in the manner of the Christian and Islamic religions: that is, it relied on winning the hearts and minds of all individuals. Even its enemies were redeemable if they were prepared to rid themselves of the old dross; since one became a communist by affiliation or conversion, the entrance gates were not barred to anyone. Nazism, however, was an ideology and a creed reserved for the Aryan elect; only they could become Nazis, through a process that involved purging impurities, recognizing common roots and reasons, and fraternizing with others on a racial basis. Aryan blood was the perennial spring feeding the vital forces of civilization, to which it was necessary to return whenever and wherever history weakened or effaced them.

In the wake of the profound crisis that shook Europe, and especially Germany, between 1914 and the early postwar years, the Nazis located the seeds of disintegration in Marxism, liberal individualism, bourgeois capitalism, egalitarian democracy (which allegedly negated the natural, biological foundation of hierarchy) and decadent art and culture; these could all be traced back to Judaism, the father of all vices and all degeneracy, which in the framework of world history was bent on destroying its sworn eternal enemy: the Aryan race. Communists believed that the epochal struggle was between capitalism and socialism, and that the proletariat was the all-important subject of Progress. For the Nazis, the struggle was between Aryanism and Judaism, and the German people, as the core and bastion of world Aryanism, were destined to guide the spiritual and political reunification of the chosen race.

This would be achieved through a return to the sources and primal values of life that history had deposited in Aryan blood at various places on earth; the time had come to build an enduring monument to Aryanism that would secure it the power of domination and eternal glory. In this vision, a thousand-year Reich would transform the Aryan people into a 'community' inspired by the supreme good of racial togetherness, under the leadership of a tightly organized hierarchy whose legitimacy rested on the right of the strong to rule over the weak. Nazism – in this respect, like communism in relation to the Soviet state – considered the German state as the national instrument in the service of a supranational mission. To the communist motto, 'Workers of the world, unite!', the Nazis counterposed their 'Aryans of the world, unite!' Whereas for Marxists history was the history of class struggle, for Nazis it was the history of race struggle; and, whereas for communists the millennium would reach its highest expression, after the abolition of capitalism and hostile classes and states, in a world order under their leadership, for Nazis the final consummation would come with the unification of all Aryans, the destruction of the enemy race and the subjugation of other inferior races.

Soviet communism saw history as a process rhythmically measured by the conquests that would mark the passage from a 'lower' stage (capitalism) to 'higher' stages (socialism and communism). Nazism, by contrast, was bound up with a static vision of 'the good', in so far as it was borne by Aryan blood with all its primal and immutable virtues. This static quality was organically linked to the idea of race as the pure fount of creative energy and vitality, from which all the true and lasting achievements of history had emanated and would continue to emanate. Hence the horror of any contamination of the blood and the injunction to stamp it out and prevent it from spreading, to end it once and for all through an Aryan politics and science that would defend racial purity, separate higher from lower races, subjugate the latter and exploit them economically, and above all wipe out the Jewish race. The Jews, it should be stressed, were seen as the enemy race: perverse, destructive of the good and beautiful, productive of all the great evils in the world. In Nazi thinking about race, for which H. S. Chamberlain was the main theoretical foundation, the Jews were the original architects of absolute evil and were therefore opposed to the Aryan custodians of absolute good in the same way that the devil was opposed to God in religious thought. The struggle between the two, which was at the basis of the vicissitudes of world history, was destined to end in a last definitive battle.

In the Nazi view of things, a tangible improvement in the human condition did not depend on universalist values, on general Progress of a unified humanity through an end to strife within and between states, on the sovereignty of a shared reason, or on the use of material resources by science and technology for the benefit of all. Rather, it depended on the rigid separation of races, the rule of Aryans over all others, a monopoly of armed might in the hands of the rulers, constant watchfulness of superior over inferior human beings, selection of an elite that would hold all power, disinfestation of unhealthy elements seeking to contaminate Aryan blood, and victory of the spirit and will to power of the elect. Science and technology would remain an instrument wholly in the service of the rulers; politics had the task of guaranteeing the new order; the economy would be organized in accordance with a racially defined hierarchy of needs; art and culture would be directed entirely towards education of the master race and the celebration and reflection of its values; ideology, morality and social customs would forge the levers for the Aryan politician, soldier, worker and citizen. The Nazi idea of improvement was thus bound up with a 'return' to atavistic roots and with surgical intervention to purge present vices and restore the ancient virtues.

5   THE SOCIAL-DEMOCRATIC VISION

While communism claimed to monopolize the idea of a necessary, guaranteed Progress and entrusted itself with the task of realizing it, a different evolution occurred in the parts of Scandinavia and the British Isles that did not endure the assaults of Bolshevism, fascism or various kinds of right-wing authoritarianism and managed to keep their democratic institutions out of danger. Here, in response to the devastating effects of the economic crisis that began in 1929 and then of the Second World War, a current of social-democratic and labour parties consolidated itself and, with the support of liberals such as John Maynard Keynes, sought to oppose communism and the Nazi-fascist threat with a strategy to reform capitalism that could afford the masses a permanent state of relative well-being or lesser ill-being. This current was driven by a mixture of idealistic and realistic motives: on the one hand, horror at the enormous suffering due to mass insecurity among a chronically underpaid or unemployed and marginalized working-class population which often faced desperate poverty and soul-destroying anxiety; on the other hand, a realization that bold social and economic reforms were needed to counter the attractiveness of the communist and fascist dictatorships, which each promised a new world on the ruins of political democracy and social-cultural pluralism. The idea, then, was to develop a reform programme that would overcome the crude, unregulated capitalism evident in the great crisis of 1929, replacing it with a publicly regulated capitalism and 'Welfare State' that would attach the working masses to representative democratic institutions and the defence of political and civil liberties. The state would assume new tasks of market regulation and take direct responsibility, even for the production of goods and services, through a publicly owned and managed financial-industrial sector. This movement at the level of ideas and politics was part of a general tendency to increase the state's role in the economy, so that a system of balances, weights and counterweights between the private and public sectors would maintain the market and economic competition but prevent the interests of the few from lording it over society. The political culture that inspired this conception had roots both in nineteenth-century democratic theorists sensitive to the social question (John Stuart Mill, Thomas H. Green, David G. Ritchie, Leonard T. Hobhouse) and in social-democratic reformists and revisionists such as Eduard Bernstein. After a number of practical applications in social-democratic governments of the 1930s, the new reformism gained strong support from the economic theories of Keynes and reached a climax in the process leading up to the creation of the Welfare State; its most important ideological manifesto and programme was the 1942 *Report* of the British economist Henry W. Beveridge, a left liberal influenced by the Webbs and Fabianism, which centred on the need for a system of social protection that would ensure full employment, permanent income support for the weakest strata of society, a guaranteed national health service, and opportunities of social promotion for the greatest possible number of people. The basic conviction behind the Beveridge Report was that full democratic citizenship could not exist without such a system of social rights safeguarded by active state intervention to establish a new equilibrium.

The 'Welfare State' took firmest hold in the postwar Labour and social-democratic governments in Britain, Sweden and Norway, but it gradually spread to all the democratic countries of Western Europe, under diverse governments and with active trade union support. Initially inspired by a convergence of left liberalism, British labourism, continental social democracy and union movements linked to the political left, the ideology of the Welfare State was later adopted also by social-Christian currents and political parties or trade unions under their influence. It thus represented a great 'compromise' between capitalism and the world of labour, based on the idea that economic policies sustained by the values of social solidarity made Progress a real possibility. Although communist parties in the West European democracies did not accept the philosophy and ideological aims of the Welfare State, regarding it as ultimately no more than a 'palliative', they too played a crucial role in its practical realization.

The main protagonists, however, were undoubtedly the social-democratic parties, even when they continued to define the ultimate goal as the overcoming of the capitalist system and the construction of a socialist society in which the means of production and exchange were owned by all. Reformist gradualism as a permanent principle and guiding value reached its highest and final expression in the German SPD's adoption of a new programme at its Bad Godesberg congress in 1959, where Marxism was put to one side in an official approval, more than half a century later, of the basic thrust of Bernstein's revisionism. The programme invoked the values of intellectual and political freedom, justice and social solidarity; it located the roots of democratic socialism in Christian ethics, humanism and classical philosophy; it appealed to a secular spirit which, safe from any temptation to impose an ultimate truth or the domination of a party-state, would give full scope to individual beliefs; it countered communist dictatorship with social-democratic loyalty to the institutions of pluralist democracy. While it defined individual rights as inviolable, it also established the supremacy of collective over individual interests and the public accountability of all powers in society.

It announced the completion of the liberal state in the social state, whose mission was to achieve, through balanced economic development and the adaptation of institutions to changes in the productive structure, the goals of full unemployment and general well-being – in accordance with the principle of competition among firms, combined with interventionist planning only when it was needed to prevent the excessive power of large corporations over their workforce and society. Private property was to be legitimate and protected, but on condition that it did not conflict with the requirements of social justice. There would thus also be a need for public enterprises, so that the private sector did not subjugate the market to particularist interests. To give a social substance to democracy, the Bad Godesberg programme asserted that workers' participation in management was an indispensable premise for the worker to become a citizen in the economic as well as the political sphere. Lastly, with regard to international relations, it gave a central place to cooperation and solidarity among different nations and states, with the United Nations Organization as the decisive instrument.

The abandonment of Marxism was evident in the SPD's rejection of class ideologies, and its definition of itself no longer as a working-class party but as a 'people's party'. Hence democracy, social, cultural and political pluralism, solidarity and social justice, an economic policy prioritizing collective needs and workforce participation in companies were the main lines of the democratic socialist programme for a comprehensive Progress that did not constrict individual rights and interests. We might say that the programme adopted by German social democracy in 1959 was a major expression of the idea of Progress whose journey had begun in the age of the Enlightenment.

Yet, a little less than twenty years later, European social democracy and its great creation, the Welfare State, entered a period of growing crisis and uncertainty as a narrowly conservative tide of neoliberalism spread outward from Britain and the United States, intent on directly challenging welfare constraints on the freedom of individual initiative and restoring an ideology of the capitalist market freed from the straitjacket of state intervention. The slogan of this victorious offensive, which took over key aspects of nineteenth-century social Darwinism, was effectively expressed in Margaret Thatcher's quip that she knew what individuals were, but not society.

6

GLOBALIZATION AND THE ETHICS OF COMPETITION

The idea of Progress, as formulated by left-liberal currents and social democracy and realized in the Welfare State, acknowledged the legacy of the Enlightenment tradition and incorporated the principle that there can be no liberty without respect for the rights and energies of individuals. But it also affirmed the principle of social justice and a set of rights without which too many individuals, because of their position in life, would remain marginalized and incapable of developing their personality or becoming citizens in the full sense. While private property, the market and freedom of action for its subjects were all recognized, it was left up to the democratically legitimated public power to ensure that resources were distributed in such a way as to combat, and ultimately to eliminate, the scourges of unemployment, low pay, inadequate health services and barriers to the development of personal energies and qualities. In short, the goal was the abolition of material and spiritual poverty, while the means to that end, in a context of pluralism, were the joint action of individuals and institutions, political, economic, trade-union and state organizations. Progress, conceived in this way, had as its primary sphere of operation the national state, and its main beneficiaries were to be social strata in need of social-cultural support and advancement, but the idea was aimed at the whole of humanity. Not by chance did 'human progress' become a familiar term.

Today, such an idea of Progress seems to have virtually faded away, at most continuing to exist as a mere residue. It retains the blazon of a decayed nobility. Progress, as a noun with a single referent, has completely given way to multiple and discrete forms of progress in various fields, and, whereas its object used to be humanity, the relevant dimensions today are those of science and technology. People constantly talk – and the reality in each case is grand enough to justify them – of 'progress' in physics, medicine, genetics, computer science, and so on, of a huge, dizzying, ceaseless accumulation of knowledge and its applications. But, unlike in those stages of the journey of Progress that aimed to express and give a meaning to the whole of human history, we are speaking now of inherently ambiguous forms of progress. For they provide new means yet are by their very nature incapable of offering any indication of how the means should be used; they serve in the same way both the good and the bad.

These more and more spectacular forms of sectoral progress have accompanied the human adventure ever since the dawn of modernity, giving the most potent confirmation of Bacon's great new insight at the beginning of the seventeenth century into the revolutionary potential of science. Nevertheless, the eighteenth-century and nine-teenth-century architects of the idea of Progress were convinced that such advances would be placed ever more efficiently at the service of a general improvement in the human condition involving a harmonious positive synthesis of morality, politics, science, technology and economics. Today, in what has come to look like a market society and not just a market economy, the huge advances in science and technology no longer have any substantive connection with the overall idea of Progress. Instead, they are quite overwhelmingly at the disposal of those who are most able to promote, fund and enjoy them.

The neoliberal impetus which drove the process of economic globalization in the last two decades of the twentieth century has created a new grammar and a new ethical, cultural, political and social syntax. In so doing, it has offered a vision of its own in complete contrast to the idea of Progress that came into being with the Enlightenment, developed with various emphases in positivism, socialism and left liberalism, and finally adopted by social-Christian currents in relation to the economy.

Neoliberal globalization, unlike the ideology that legitimates it, is guided not by the initiatives of individuals but by those of the dominant subjects in finance and industry. These subjects bend nation-states to their own requirements – states which are by now largely emptied of sovereignty, in a context where systems of 'national economy' are in evident crisis – and raise market freedom to a supreme value and goal at the same time that they abuse monopolistic practices and get along perfectly well with any protectionist barriers that are to their advantage. These tendencies represent a distortion of the idea of Progress, since they measure the improvement of humanity by the yardstick offered by economic magnates whose main aim is to augment their own income (which has indeed increased in recent decades quite disproportionately to the income of dependent workers). It is a world where, even in the most developed countries, the right to work is considered the product of obsolete ideologies and a sense of insecurity is spreading together with precarious forms of employment; where countries caught up in rapid economic growth, especially China and India, witness the development of monstrous inequalities among different social strata; where some regions boom while others often remain impoverished and suffer unbridled exploitation of labour, because trade union leaders are trampled on with impunity and even children can be forced into slave labour; where the overall gap between the most developed and the most backward areas remains abysmal and the greatest attention is focused on the requirements of profit and consumption. In these conditions, the very goal of the comprehensive development of humanity can have no meaning. Individuals, groups and countries divide up into 'winners' and 'losers', into those who win the wager for life and those who lose it.

Neoliberalism, whose great chorus leaders in the 1980s were the conservatives Margaret Thatcher and Ronald Reagan, programmatically besieged and battered the pillars of the 'social state'. Social rights were once again counterposed to the rights of the individual, and public regulation to market freedom; the Welfare State was seen as the illegitimate result of harmful state encroachment on the economy, the cause of unacceptable instability in public finances, an incentive to welfare 'scroungers', and a major obstacle to more responsible attitudes that embraced risk and competition as the very spirit of an innovative market economy. Spurring themselves on with attacks on indubitable managerial failures in the existing welfare systems, the new conservatives set themselves the aim of throwing out the baby with the bathwater.

The neoliberal offensive was greatly assisted by the stagnation and collapse of the Soviet system, the highest expression of bureaucratic statism, since the dictatorship that had claimed to be the pinnacle of social and political progress ended up producing an epochal disaster for itself, for the peoples caught up in it and for the international left of which it claimed to be the largest and by far the most important part. But the offensive also deeply shook European social democracy, which, though victorious in the confrontation with communism that had begun in 1917, was gravely weakened in the face of the new conservative governments and policies. Its first difficulty was to find some way of coming to terms with the fate of an economic model based upon a strong public sector and the centrality of large factories, whose marked exhaustion had been gradually reducing the number of workers with fixed jobs and a political reference point in the parties of the left and associated trade unions. The second difficulty was linked to the vast network of services that had begun to flourish on the basis of a workforce lacking traditional job security and the defensive props of the welfare system, which did not have the sense of collective solidarity typical of factory workers and showed little inclination for political or trade-union activity. The third difficulty came from the conservatives' determination to slash the fiscal burden on high-income groups especially, so as to release financial resources for the private sector. The watchword that the market economy and society issued to individual workers was: 'Look out for yourself and trust in the divine hand of the market.' In place of common Progress under public direction, conservative neoliberal ideology insisted that it was mainly up to individuals to provide for themselves by taking the opportunities offered by a theoretically free market (even if, in reality, it was the multinationals and their managerial elites who laid down the law).

Of course, conservative governments did not simply abolish the institutions of the Welfare State, since that would have led to a real unravelling of the fabric of society, but they did gradually render them blunt and sterile, with the long-term aim of uprooting the values at the heart of the welfare system and turning it into little more than 'public charity'. This dealt a body blow to social democracy, and in some cases – most notably, Tony Blair's New Labour – it ended up acting as the stooge of neoliberalism. But one vigorous and successful barrier remained in the social-democratic parties of Scandinavia, which put up significant resistance to the main tendency. In fact, they forcefully revived a strategy of high taxation in return for efficient cutting-edge state welfare services, within a general productive context that showed it was possible to face international competition through a great innovative drive in high-tech sectors and the regulation of relations among the different parts of society in a market setting.

The globalization promoted by neoliberals and neoconservatives involves a curious paradox: it is one mode of dissolving the idea of Progress variously developed by Enlightenment thought, positivism and socialism, but at the same time it appears to realize some of the key goals of all those movements. The Enlightenment looked forward to the global spread of knowledge and cosmopolitan culture, and globalization is spreading knowledge and culture in the world as never before. Positivism sought to establish the dominance of science and technology, and globalization is giving it a scale that knows no bounds. Socialism set itself the task of achieving political and economic internationalism, and globalization seems to be doing this at breakneck speed. At the same time, however, globalization advances these objectives by giving them a completely different character from that which Enlightenment thought, positivism and socialism wished to stamp on them. It aims at the universalization of values, yet they are Western values which, if necessary, have to be spread through violence. It celebrates the triumph of science and technology, yet makes them strictly dependent on the interests of the great financial and industrial power centres. It gives free rein to political and economic internationalism, yet does so with the aim of reducing states to subaltern agencies of capitalism. In short, it brings well-being by the standards of the market instead of the well-being of humanity; rule by economic oligarchies instead of democratic states; precarious employment instead of stable jobs; rights for individuals mainly defined by the purchasing power of their income, instead of rights that promote the all-round personalities of individual citizens; and, instead of the ideal of social justice, general competition leading to the victory of some over others as the highest manifestation of justice (an ethic of 'let everyone grab what they can make their own'). So, if neoliberal globalization means the dissolution of Progress, should we give up the whole idea? What is left of humanity if it entrusts its own future, and its prospects of improvement, to competition among individual and collective subjects inspired by an acute and often morally ruthless form of social neo-Darwinism? Is a globalization different from the conservative neoliberal form possible or even conceivable?

7

DEMOCRACY: BETWEEN VALUE AND REALITY

In all versions of the idea of Progress, the goal of achieving ever better forms of government has always occupied a central place; we may say that it is a necessity inherent in the idea. We have already had occasion to note that the ideologies of Progress presupposed a combination of ethical, political, cultural and social improvement. But the relationship with democracy was not altogether clear. The Enlightenment thinkers were in favour of reforms but were not democrats. Their main reference values were the moral and intellectual liberty of individuals, tolerance, a rejection of oppressive and levelling forms of power, and the development of civilized customs. When they tried to identify the subjective agents of reform, they mainly looked to the sovereigns who introduced, or said they wanted to introduce, it. In an age that they considered still too much in thrall to the legacies of the past, in which the masses seemed and indeed were shut up in their spiritual and material backwardness, they placed their hopes in elites capable of recognizing the importance of reforms and steering humanity intellectually and politically along the path of improvement. The democracy advocated in great solitude by Rousseau was either opposed outright or considered, among others by the Genevan himself, as an ideal model or yardstick, a utopia achievable only in a

small political community. The most advanced political
horizon was the constitutional rule of law (to protect civil
society and its freedoms from arbitrary and despotic
power) and a system in which political participation was
limited to the upper and middle strata of society through
their representative institutions. Comtean positivists as
well as socialists of the Jacobin school imagined, for their
part, that 'sociocracy' or the dictatorship of a conscious
revolutionary minority would open the way to Progress.

Democracy powerfully joined the mainstream of
Progress in and after 1848–9, bringing to light fundamental differences between the positions of the republican
movement and those of Marxist socialism (which
appeared on the scene precisely in 1848). The appeal to
democracy as a vehicle of Progress was the common
denominator, but the ways in which they understood and
sought to achieve it seemed rather different. For it was
one thing to conceive democracy in a cross-class perspective, and another to conceive it in a class perspective. The
former tendency thought of democracy in terms of
universal suffrage, a constituent assembly to set up representative institutions, freedom of association and political
and social pluralism; the latter envisaged that a process of
'permanent revolution' would ensure the passage from
bourgeois to proletarian institutions, from capitalism to
socialism – in short, a transition from bourgeois
democracy, seen as a container or terrain for class conflict,
to the abolition of private property via a distinctively proletarian democracy or a dictatorship of the proletarian
majority. The two democracies joined up and even
merged with each other in a determination to combat
either absolute monarchs and their aristocratic-oligarchic
supporters or new bourgeois oligarchies hostile to mass
political participation and working-class freedom of association. They were united against the old world, but

differed profoundly in their perspectives for the future. Mazzini was a typical representative of the first tendency, Marx and Engels of the second.

It is important to note that both non-socialist democrats and democratic socialists regarded the state as an indispensable instrument for the organization of society. But a third current also vigorously entered the field of political and social conflict at that time: anarchism, whose most important exponents were Proudhon and later Bakunin, opposed the subjugation of society head-on and called for the mobilization of all the oppressed – not only the workers, as Marxists did, but also poor peasants, marginal strata and deracinated intellectuals. The anarchists were resolute opponents of democrats of various stripes, because their aim was to overthrow any kind of state and political order. As they saw things, it was necessary to leap without further ado from institutions that sanctioned political oppression and economic exploitation to a system of self-management presided over by free individuals in a relationship of social and economic cooperation. They rejected the rule of the aristocracy and bourgeoisie, capitalism and any kind of statism, even socialist. In their eyes, socialists and especially Marxists – whose idea of future society also, however, involved self-management without a state, money or division of labour – preached a false gospel when they argued that dictatorship, political force and statist collectivization of the means of production would be required to reach the goal: false, because the means would swallow up the end, leading not to abolition of the state and the withering away of dictatorship, but to permanent and general enslavement to the state, both political and economic. And yet, however great their differences, non-socialist democrats, democratic socialists and anarchists shared a conception of the future as Progress and, in both theory and practice, advocated mass participation as essential to decisions concerning the structure of society.

In rejecting any involvement in existing institutions, the anarchists excluded themselves from the march of the masses towards democracy. But democratic gains – extended suffrage, freedom of political and trade union association, all political and civil rights beginning with women's rights, and a range of new social rights – characterized the history of the Western world from the second half of the nineteenth century, becoming an essential component of the idea of Progress as they went through a dense cycle of ebb and flow, steps forward and steps back, according to the varied geography of states and nations. The main agents in this trend were the cultural and political currents of left liberalism, radicalism and democratic republicanism, then with ever greater weight the socialist parties, and finally, between the late-nineteenth and early-twentieth centuries, the currents and parties of Christian-Democratic inspiration. Political and labour struggles, together with the activities of union federations and cooperatives, tore the working masses out of their traditionally passive and marginal condition and educated them in democratic participation.

The socialist parties of Western Europe, the chief protagonists in the emergence of the masses on to the public stage during the sixty years before the First World War, were for a long time convinced that 'true' democracy would begin only with the end of capitalism and the coming of socialism, since only the leap from one form of society to another would make democracy itself 'substantive'. In the countries with representative liberal institutions, however, the socialist parties were increasingly influenced by the trade unions to adjust to the rules and forms of activity of the parliamentary system, to struggle for an extension of the suffrage, to improve conditions at the workplace, and in general to wrest new political and social reforms at a gradual pace. So, even when reformism was still considered a means rather than an end, it continued to sink deep roots in society in a contradictory and far from linear way. Democratic participation and social reformism came to be seen as part and parcel of the road to greater Progress. The socialist parties and unions felt themselves to be fully engaged in this movement of society that assigned the masses to organizations under the direction of cadres and elites – although, importantly for the education and advancement of the masses, those elites were largely open to the recruitment of people from a popular background. For the first time in the history of Europe, such elements had a way of gaining significant access to political leadership roles, and indeed many ordinary members of the working classes rose to the top of parties or trade unions and entered Parliament. This was the context in which reformism grew continually stronger, despite the opposition of those who limited themselves to rejecting it 'in principle' and in their own conduct.

It has been said that the interwar period presaged a major eclipse for the conception of Progress as incremental gains. During those years, liberal democracy and reformist socialism underwent such a grave crisis that they were in danger of being swept away by forces which either rejected democracy as such or thought of it as a unitary 'power' of the popular masses and their authoritarian leaders in opposition to cultural, political and social pluralism – forces, therefore, which sought to establish a regime, an emergency dictatorship, capable of concentrating all power in a single bundle or *fascio*. This objective was shared by communists on the one hand, and by fascists, Nazis and various authoritarian right-wing extremists on the other. The democratic systems of Britain, France and a few smaller countries withstood the rising tide, but they resisted weakly and ineffectively. In the 1930s, when Europe was simultaneously gripped by the effects of economic crisis and the rise of Soviet communism, Nazism and fascism, the democracy of the British or French seemed and was unglamorous, opaque, old and creaking, incapable of reacting. Hopes of change, innovation or improvement shifted decisively towards the totalitarian dictatorships, which promised a red or a black millennium. The British Labour Party was drained as a governmental force, while the Conservatives were so concerned at the possibility of communist expansion that they became more than tolerant towards Nazism and fascism and surrendered one position after another until September 1939, when they themselves were gripped by the throat and finally compelled to react.

French democracy, deeply divided and under internal attack from the nationalist right, authoritarian clericalism, crypto-fascism and communism, also proved incapable of opposing, when it still had the strength, either the arrogant Nazi foreign policy or the spread of fascistic and anti-Semitic tendencies within French society and the growing influence of ultra-conservative strata determined to defend their interests by any means. The depth of divisions in the country became evident during the Popular Front governments of 1936–8, which tried to set a counter-tendency in motion; the Socialist Léon Blum had to bow before the 'strike of capital' – in effect, a strike by French democracy, which in the hands of Daladier went on to accept the Munich capitulation. The military defeat came in 1940, reflecting the state of a country that no longer had the political or moral resources to put up solid resistance to the German armies. The French collapse, like Italy in 1919–22 and Germany in 1919–32, was a classic case of a democracy corroded in the depths of its being: that is, of a formally democratic system in which too many social and political forces withheld mutual recognition, sought to overwhelm one another, did not share the same values, and did not accept democratic institutions or their ground rules as a common public space. Such attitudes went a long way back in these and other countries of liberal Europe and were quite widespread in the political geography of the continent.

Only in America, at the time of Europe's lurch toward totalitarianism and authoritarianism and the weakening of its democratic regimes, did democracy prove capable of standing firm and rejuvenating itself under the strong and innovative leadership of Franklin D. Roosevelt. He had the capacity to give fresh hope and energy to his country, after it had been plunged into a state of acute social, political and ideological uncertainty following the Crash of 1929. Roosevelt's America was the only major country in the Western world where the idea of possible Progress found refuge and new vigour. But the United States was too remote from European experience: it did not speak to the exhausted European democracies, nor was it able to inject new energy into them in a decade dominated by the tyrannies of Hitler, Stalin and Mussolini. Moreover, both fascists and communists looked on America with disdain, convinced that the New Deal could do no more than usher in a crisis that would sooner or later carry that country too towards fascism or communism.

Whatever their limits, liberal institutions and the advance of democracy in Europe from the second half of the nineteenth century down to the 1920s brought with them important social, civil and political gains; they tore millions of human beings out of supine inertia, mobilized them and educated them to fight for their rights, raised them to a higher level of intellectual and material life, and generally marked an important stage in the tortured and conflictual course of Progress.

After the end of the Second World War, despite the defeat of fascism, the cause of democracy appeared extremely insecure in continental Europe. The Iberian peninsula was still under the rule of fascistic regimes; France was emerging from the collaborationist regime of Marshal Pétain, which had proved to have deep and extensive roots; a newly redivided Germany, reeling from the material effects of defeat and the huge support it had given to Hitler, was placed under an occupation regime in both its eastern and western parts; Italy had behind it a past as the birthplace of fascism as well as the wrenching experience of civil war in 1943–5; Greece was prey to internal convulsions; Eastern Europe and the Balkans were rapidly going communist and would soon have a vast network of dictatorial regimes posing as 'people's democracies'.

The revival of democracy in Western Europe was closely bound up with the victory of the United States and Great Britain. The former powerfully asserted itself on the postwar scene with the legacy of Roosevelt, who in the thirties had revitalized American society and restructured the state's relationship with capitalism and the world of labour; the latter, having turned the page on Chamberlain's capitulationism and resisted the Nazi armies with indomitable courage, brought to power a Labour government and laid the basis for a welfare system that would involve a new political and social contract between the social partners and set an example to other West European countries. Thus, New Deal America and Labour's welfare Britain were able to guide the reconstruction of Western Europe on the twin bases of military victory and a progressive political-social programme materially aided by America's vast economic power. This combination erected a hugely effective barrier to the expansion of communism in the West. In France and Italy, which still

had the weight of their Pétainist or fascist past, the rebuild-
ing of democracy was also able to count on energies
generated by the Resistance, which, though deeply divided
in its ideologies and aspirations, shared a common desire
to restore political and civil liberties, representative
institutions and political and cultural pluralism.

Such were the resources for democratic renewal within
the context of postwar economic reconstruction. And the
pro-Soviet left, while believing in and hoping for the final
worldwide victory of the Soviet system, had to adjust to
the situation and even become an active and essential part
of it by playing the democratic game. In West Germany,
the rebirth of democracy occurred in the harshest conditions, against the backdrop of a material and spiritual
cemetery. It was necessary to find roots in pre-Nazi history
and it was from these that the two great mass parties,
Social Democracy and Christian Democracy, and a liberal
party re-emerged in a country freed from the hold of the
military and bureaucratic castes. The majority of the
German people was thus able to find a way forward again
in democracy, on more solid ground than the fragile, dis-
jointed and tormented Weimar Republic had been able to
provide.

In most of Western Europe, the first decade after the
war was one of major economic and social development,
enough to justify the belief that 'possible' Progress had
resumed its forward march. Change was pursued through
the method of reforms, political power was limited, and
democratic participation was greatly enhanced by female
suffrage in countries where it had not existed before. The
Welfare State gradually strengthened itself as a diffuse
objective, science and technology developed in leaps and
bounds, and the rapid and imposing material construction contradicted the widespread mood of postwar
pessimism. Another highly important element in the

democratic countries of Europe was the gradually spreading sense of a common affiliation, of the desirability of a process of regional integration such as that which got off the ground in the late 1940s. The combination of factors underpinning the idea of Progress may be said to have become active once again. The ideological, cultural, political and social contradictions and contrasts remained profound, but their effects were contained within certain limits. In Italy and France, which had the strongest communist parties linked to the Soviet world as well as associated trade union movements, the sometimes acute political and economic conflicts never left the bounds of legality; and, despite the Cold War raging at international level, hostility to 'bourgeois democracy' did not induce these parties to leave its stage during the decade of reconstruction, partly as a result of the fact that surging economic growth created insurmountable obstacles in practice to any anti-systemic strategy and perspective. Indeed, the ideological and social conflicts were a decisive spur to participation in the system of party politics, and the mass parties also played a positive role in the education of citizens. The communists themselves, tightly organized by their apparatuses, remained in a state of ideological subordination and veritable blindness with regard to the reality of the Soviet world, but they were also in the front line of labour and civil rights struggles or activity in local government and the cooperative sector, exercising a dialectically vital function in the whole question of democratic participation. What emerged was a kind of perfected replica of the 'integration' process of the late-nineteenth and early-twentieth centuries, which had affected the mainstream of (ideologically still revolutionary) socialist currents.

In the forty years following the Second World War, the countries of Western Europe – joined in 1974–5 by

Portugal and Spain, then newly emerging from authoritarian regimes – experienced a 'party democracy' that was rather more fully fledged than it had been before. Political parties formed the link between electors and elected in the network of representative institutions stretching from Parliament down to local councils; they stimulated the energies of the competing forces through their own party organization, membership meetings, political rallies and mass demonstrations; they channelled consent and mobilized it for elections. In all this mass activity, the trade unions played a central role alongside the parties, so that in Europe, in comparison with America, democracy was considerably more ideological and had stronger links to specific sectors of society. The two main US parties were certainly not ignorant of ideological and programmatic conflict, but they were interclass formations unlike their more class-inflected counterparts across the Atlantic. The parties of the European left, in particular, typically had a base among industrial workers and more generally among dependent low-income earners. Beyond their national diversity, the political systems in democratic Europe achieved three essential objectives: to secure effective political representation of classes and social groups, to keep political and social differences within the bounds of constitutional legality, and to provide less well-off strata of society with better living conditions as a result of long-term economic growth. There was no lack of pauses, slowdowns and even reverses. But the striking major tendency, within a framework of democratic institutions, was for a liberal matrix to be shared in practice even by parties and currents that pursued other models and expected them to become reality at some time in the future.

All this involved actual Progress based on the convergence of: (1) a long phase of capitalist expansion;

(2) democratic institutions which – despite severe tensions and acute crisis in the 1960s and 1970s, especially in France (subversive right-wing colonialist elements), Italy (subversive actions by terrorist movements) and Greece (the dictatorship of the colonels) – seemed quite secure in comparison with the interwar period; and (3) improved working-class living conditions, in the absence of economic crises comparable to those of the past. Democracy in Western Europe, resting upon what has been called a 'social-democratic compromise' linking capitalist economy and welfare system, proved capable of handling political and social conflicts through negotiation and effective reforms.

Meanwhile, the 'necessary' progress guaranteed by 'Marxist science', and controlled by ruling communist elites under the aegis of a new, socialist democracy, descended from greatest illusion to total disillusionment, from absolute certainty to incurable confusion. In the countries of 'actually existing socialism', the Tables of Progress were not negotiable; the regime imposed them as untouchable dogmas. For nearly thirty years after 1945, the countries where the communists ruled in much the same way as they had in isolated Russia sought to confiscate the idea of Progress for themselves. The Soviet Union, having subdued Nazi Germany, constructed around itself a band of countries in which China towered above the others; Marxism-Leninism seemed destined to spread to the rest of the world, as the universalist mission of the 'revolutionary proletariat' seemed to acquire greater credibility. Communism claimed to be an invincible combination of the best political governance, a public ethic superior to all others, and unbroken development of the economy, science and technology. When the Soviet Union began the conquest of space in the late 1950s, and in the first part of the next decade seemed close to its obsessional goal of overtaking the United States, it seemed to have shown that it held firmly in its hands the torch of human Progress.

Triumphalism was also the dominant note in the other great communist power, China, and elsewhere in the communist world. However, the reality behind the appearances was quite different. Science, technology and economics in these countries were mainly placed in the service of a military effort which, given the exigencies of the contest with the wealthier West, ate up resources and distorted the development of society; socialist democracy was a propaganda slogan providing cover for an oppressive political despotism that went through tighter or looser periods but did not change its structures as one ruler succeeded another; unlimited statism made society barren and ended up destroying it; the repressive system clapped a mantle of fear on people and their conscience; periodic campaigns to mobilize society for some breathtaking objective – Khrushchev's 'conquest of virgin lands' and Mao's 'great leap forward' and 'cultural revolution' were major examples in the post-Stalin period – had the effect of exhausting the population and, in the case of China, led to massive disasters with millions of casualties. By the mid-1960s the Soviet Union had entered the period of stagnation which, at the end of the 1980s, culminated in the collapse of the regime and its East European empire. China, in seeking a way out, had to make a dramatic volte-face in the 1980s and ultimately embrace that unprecedented mixture of capitalism and communist power which Mao had tried in vain to avert. Thus, in the end, the myth of communism as the victorious incarnation of necessary and guaranteed Progress led to the total and irreversible discrediting of communism itself. The dictatorship that claimed to be the highest form of democracy went bankrupt after stifling the energies of the peoples subject to it.

While communism completed its ideological and political parabola with the collapse that ingloriously terminated its claim to embody Progress, the same period witnessed the growing exhaustion of the Western 'compromise' between capital and labour, which, in contrast to communism, had represented the expression of a problematic, uneven Progress, subject to alternations, to ebbs and flows, but which, at the level of national states, had brought about a truly remarkable improvement in the living conditions of workers.

There now came one of those epochal turns that literally change the world, altering the rhythms of time and the value of space, and the velocity and intensity with which people make use of them. The geopolitical map was redrawn as major players disappeared and global power was redistributed, with the rise of strong new states, the association of smaller with larger ones, and the formation of new spheres of hegemony; classes and social strata from the old generation lost some of their importance as new strata appeared on the scene; the productive forces were restructured through qualitative changes in technology and at the level of work and company organization; transfers of culture, technology and goods hugely expanded and intensified; and the resources produced in this way were reallocated both vertically and horizontally. All in all, then, the change that took place in the last two decades of the twentieth century, with the advent of what has been called 'globalization', appears comparable in significance to those that occurred between the fifteenth and sixteenth centuries and between the eighteenth and nineteenth centuries.

The process had objective foundations that cannot be disregarded, but like all similar processes it allowed for various options and could have been 'managed' in different ways and with different outcomes. The main objective factors were: the declining weight of large factories and of working-class concentrations in often gigantic productive units; the information 'revolution' and massive deployment of automation; the resulting application of new productive technology; somewhat faster corporate turnover due to the greatly accelerated pace of technological innovation and a need to chase after consumers in a market that had expanded as never before in history; the race of international finance and industry to invest in every corner of the world, where profitability pressures mostly threw into ever deeper crisis the traditional 'national economic systems' of individual countries; the unprecedented role played by the major financial and industrial power centres in deciding on relocation of the productive forces; the agreements in every continent to form vast economic cooperation and free trade areas. All this developed together with a redrawing of the geopolitical map of the world, whose main protagonists are currently the United States, the European Union, the Russian Federation, Japan, China and India.

The type of economic development that began in the late eighteenth century and came to an end in the last two decades of the twentieth involved a close interlinking of the national and international. But the main players configuring the international space had their chief interests and their most important operational and productive decision-making centres within the frontiers of particular countries. The world market, taking shape largely as a result of their operations and expansion, was anything but open. It had to be conquered and defended piece by piece, often literally in an environment of high conflict; armies gladly opened a path for the initiatives of national capitalists or state managers (after the emergence of state-controlled economic sectors in the communist countries and elsewhere), and blocked the path to those of other countries. Free trade was promoted by states which, like Britain in the decades following its industrial revolution, held an overwhelming technological, industrial, financial and commercial superiority, but was opposed by others which, having achieved an adequate degree of self-sufficiency, felt a great need for barriers to protect their national market and to ensure their own further development. Internationally, then, the principle of competition was by no means taken for granted or peacefully accepted. It operated in a limited and intermittent manner and could not displace the role of individual states, which, according to their level of development and particular needs, promoted free trade or protectionism and geared their foreign policy either to peaceful aims or to commercial warfare that sometimes escalated into armed hostilities.

In a long wave that was already well-defined in the last decade of the nineteenth century and lasted for a hundred years or more, the state, especially in Europe, accelerated and deepened its role in economic regulation by taking responsibility for essential public services and, through key industrial and financial corporations, for certain sectors that private initiative was covering either poorly or scarcely at all. Economic statism, in the guise of a regulatory and entrepreneurial state, reached a peak in Western countries in the 1930s, in response to the great crisis of 1929, but acquired its most radical form (that is, general collectivization of the means of production) in the Soviet Union and other communist countries; the effects of the First World War had already given a push in this direction. So, the state – leaving aside here the omnipresent and omnipotent communist state, which excluded all other players – did not limit its role to the economy but intervened in a large network of relations. In the eighteenth and nineteenth centuries it had taken charge of mass (or, in a significant new usage, 'public') education, of the policing of relations between capital and labour and the whole area of political, trade-union, health-insurance and cooperative associations. Then, in a movement pioneered by Bismarck in the 1880s, the state felt impelled for reasons of internal order and national unity to introduce the kind of social legislation that culminated in the welfare system, both to have healthier, more motivated workers and to bind citizens more tightly to existing institutions. The chief agency in all these decisions was the national state, and wherever it acquired liberal-democratic foundations the decisions were directly influenced by social and political struggles on its territory. Thus, the national state occupied a commanding position with regard to the economic system and political and social relations; it established and regulated the rights and duties of its citizens. In short, the economy was a system subject to the national political authority, and, although this was quite sensitive to the interests of private industry and finance, it had the formal and substantive powers to override them; it also had to take account of the interests expressed by political organizations and trade unions in the world of work.

Globalization has been more and more altering, to the point of overturning, relations between the industrial-financial power centres and the national state, with profound consequences for the effectiveness of the mechanisms of democracy. The first to be put in question, even before the democratic system, is the state *tout court*. Having emerged in the modern age as a supreme unifying and disciplining centre within its own borders, a general power capable of controlling and, if necessary, stifling particular powers, the state now finds itself largely emptied of its traditional attributes (above all in the economy) and essentially reduced to administrative functions. The dominant centres of finance and industry, reaching as never before across frontiers in a global market, are able to establish plutocracy at the heart of government, setting and imposing its own conditions; in many cases it can assist the formation, or provoke the fall, of governments according to their popularity rating.

Conservative neoliberals have used the free market as a sharp weapon against 'invasive' and 'stifling' state controls, gradually demonstrating that theirs is an ideology inspired by social Darwinism. Their aim is to clear the way for industrial and financial 'neofeudalism' and the 'plutocratization' of government – as we have clearly seen in the most powerful country in the world, under the administration of George W. Bush, where big capital has exploited globalization with unprecedented force. The forward march of plutocracy was made considerably easier by the collapse of communism in the Soviet Union and its hollowing out in China. For events in those two huge countries in the last two decades have provided the most solid terrain for economic neofeudalism. A form of capitalism has appeared there which, in its extreme manifestations, deserves the name 'wild' that has been applied to it: power centres subjugate and even ransack the economy, producing huge wealth for the new plutocrats and dire poverty for whole strata of the population left to fend for themselves without a minimum guaranteed income, health services, social rights or trade-union protection – a vast pool of labour at the mercy of global financial and industrial capital, which ruthlessly draws on it to the point of reducing millions of young children to a new slavery. Similar points can be made about many other countries in Asia and Latin America. The last (but only relative) bulwark is the European Union, where, in varying degrees and with varying characteristics, political organizations and trade unions still resist the power of the

international plutocracy by fighting to defend the Welfare
State and social rights.

It has become ever clearer that the dominant centres of
international economic power take decisions of huge
importance for the lives of individuals, social groups and
whole nations, while democratic political institutions,
confined to the level of the nation-state, have no effective
means of controlling them. By an intrinsic logic, the
activity of the plutocracy is dominated by a quest for
higher profits and a wish to build a social environment
pliant to its interests, lifestyles, values and tastes; these
requirements dictate which human material is used or
discarded at any given time, with no concern for the basic
need of workers and everyone else to have adequate
resources for their span of life on earth. Such matters lie
outside the calculations relevant to the functioning of an
efficient economy.

The cornerstone of neoliberal ideology is that a free
market creates the greatest opportunities, that it is up to
individuals to grasp them as best they can, and that this
ensures the optimum distribution of collective resources.
In the real world, however, things are quite different. In
the first place, a market dominated by the great economic
magnates is by no means wide open to individual initiative; indeed, it is subject to the action and control of those
magnates, who will opt for any strategy capable of
shielding them from competition or, when it suits them,
altering its mechanisms. Both in the early-developed
countries and in those such as Russia, China and India
that have more recently been dragged into the capitalist
vortex, there has been an accelerated and hitherto unparalleled concentration of wealth in the hands of financial
oligarchies, while the middle and *a fortiori* the lower levels
of society have seen their income levels seriously eroded.
At the same time, although relative positions on the map

of development and underdevelopment have sometimes changed, the scissors between rich and poor countries remains a central factor. Nor, of course, is the expanding power of the plutocracy limited to the distribution of material resources; it invades and shapes every sphere of society. As it bends the labour force to its will, it makes use of natural resources with no heed for environmental sustainability: the supreme goal is to maximize production and consumption as the basis for higher profits, and so the ever graver warnings of an impending ecological catastrophe fall on deaf ears. Hence the inexorable march of destruction – the disappearing forests, the contaminated water, air and soil. And, while the plutocrats daily sing the praises of democracy (with the present exception of China, where unbridled capitalism goes hand in hand with political dictatorship), they actively seek to increase their control over the mass media so as to create the greatest possible support for their interests and objectives, transforming the mass of citizens into consumers of a policy that plutocracy decisively shapes. Evidently its intention is not to abolish the forms of democracy but to hollow them out by reducing political power to an instrument in its hands.

This process is well under way, but it still encounters strong resistance. First, we should bear in mind that the plutocracy is not a united or homogeneous entity: its ethics, modes of conduct and tools of action are largely the same, but its corporate and market objectives often diverge quite widely. In many cases these centres agree among themselves how to divide up spheres of influence, but in many others they are unable to do so because their particular interests conflict with one another – and one effect of this is to limit their capacity to subjugate cultural, political and social forces and institutions. Second, the activities of the plutocracy generate countervailing forces and tendencies which, even if they do not now seem capable of offering effective alternatives, continue to offer a significant degree of resistance. In the Western democracies, despite the growth of plutocratic influence, pluralism still operates in politics, the party system, the media, ideas and society in general; movements and organizations are active which refuse to accept neoconservatism, social neo-Darwinism, consumerism and environmental degradation as simple facts of life; and, as we have seen, some governments, especially the Scandinavian social democrats, show that it is possible to reconcile scientific-technological innovation and international market competitiveness with an effective defence of social rights and protection for the weakest strata of society.

The contest is thus still open between the two major tendencies of the epoch. On the one hand, a neo-Darwinian vision links development to the primacy of powerful economic interests and the subordination of politics to their ends. But another trend – rather weaker, it is true – rejects such a course and sees the basis of Progress in a combination of moral education, democratic government, non-predatory use of material resources, a socially fairer distribution of wealth, and the removal of external constraints that humiliate and oppress the personalities of too many individuals.

At this point the question arises as to whether we can and should give up the idea of Progress. What would a world be like that did without it? And, if we still need it, how should we conceive of it?

The twentieth century was a great burial ground for ideas and bodies. In keeping with the incredible acceleration of history, far beyond anything in previous epochs, it witnessed the huge bloodbaths of international, civil and ideological wars, in the name of authoritarian or dictatorial forms of power; the domination of one class, race or religion over others, in opposition to liberty and democracy; it saw the fall of the great Chinese, Tsarist, Ottoman, Austro-Hungarian, German and Japanese empires; and the rise and fall of ambitious 'new orders', whether communist or National Socialist, intended to change the world once and for all. In this vast cemetery, the idea of Progress – rooted in the seventeenth-century scientific revolution, eighteenth-century Enlightenment culture and nineteenth-century positivism – was laid to rest both by those who consciously rejected it and by those who had first undergone its moulding influence and then gravely deformed it. On the one hand, various worshippers of the 'will to power' poured scorn and trampled on the idea of Progress; it came under attack from radical critics of pacifism, cosmopolitanism and humanitarianism; from those who denied the possibility of rational moral universalism and cooperation among nations and cultures; and from advocates of an aggressive vitalism based on the opposition between strong and weak, winners and losers, superior and inferior beings or peoples. On the other hand, it was disfigured and discredited by those who made of it an instrument of oppression and a political religion in the service of dictatorship. In the twentieth century, the great enemies of the humanist idea of Progress were the various regimes based on political and economic oppression, fascistic state-worship, totalitarian Nazism and communism. Today its main enemies are plutocratic capitalism and – at the extreme – the various kinds of religious fundamentalism (the Islamic example being the most intense and widespread), which call for a restored social order to be dictated by their sacred texts. So, if we consign the idea of Progress to the dustbin of history, we leave the field to a struggle between two forces: those who advocate tumultuous change, with no guidance as to how to achieve a better, more humane political, civil and social order; and those who, competing fanatically and intolerantly with one another, uphold past traditions, cultures, mentalities and lifestyles, dreaming of an impossible restoration that would impose the tables of the Koran, the Bible or some other holy book as the legal framework for social coexistence, politics and customs. The former embody a 'soulless' modernity, the latter an obscurantist fight-back of the soul.

In order to understand whether Progress can resume its course and again become a regulative ideal of human action, we need to present some preliminary thoughts about how humanity might conceive the relationship between the present and the future. Without a doubt, some groups of individuals display a distinct indifference to the future of the world. In the motley human universe, there is no lack of people who hold life in contempt, care little about what might happen and even feel driven by a kind of death wish, a sense of *cupio dissolvi*; or of people who, possessed by a religious faith that leads them to see themselves and others as beings whose real destiny is not fulfilled on this earth, await or even long for a regenerative collapse. But, of course, the vast majority of humanity wishes not only to go on living but to improve its material and spiritual conditions of life, whatever obstacles stand in the way. Today, there are basically two options open to us.

The first is to follow passively the neoconservative and neoliberal course, which, as a kind of new 'objectivism', defines itself as the only viable path to the overall improvement of humanity. A sworn enemy of communism, it nevertheless presents significant analogies with communism's declared monopoly on the truths of economic and social science, its promise of radiant horizons to all countries if only they follow its patent recipes, and its claim to be the only formula that offers the best opportunities to all aspirants. After all, communism too proclaimed itself to be the only movement capable of bringing freedom and prosperity to the peoples of the world, to workers and ultimately all individuals. It had a huge reputation, and in the 1930s – when the capitalist world was reeling from the mass unemployment and poverty that followed the 1929 Crash – it claimed, like neoliberalism today, to have found the only formula for success. Yet, beneath the ideological mantle of communist objectivism lay the reality of unbridled subjectivism, rather like what today is hidden behind neoliberal objectivism. In both cases, the surest outcome is to provide the power elites with a way of controlling society and resource distribution that promotes their own interests.

In the communist world, the subject that shaped society and held it in thrall was the single Party; in the neoliberal world it is the plutocracy. The former exercised control over the productive forces through their collectivization, sought to use state power as the means to its own power, and invoked communist equality as its legitimating ideology; the latter subordinates economic and social development to the dominant centres of finance and industry and, as far as possible, the state itself to its own ambitions and interests, while invoking as its legitimating ideology the opportunities that free market competition supposedly offers to all those capable of seizing them. In communist society, the myth of equality covered up the harshly oligarchic power of a political-bureaucratic minority that used the economy as its instrument; in neoconservative society, the myth of maximum freedom through the market conceals a mechanism that increases inequalities of power and income, exalts the predatory acquisition of goods as a primary social value, turns business magnates into a race of overlords protected by wealth and shameless displays of material well-being that are the envy of others, and considers workers' rights an improper and uneconomic burden on the accumulation process. Whereas the communist oligarchy preached the marvels of state ownership and planning, the plutocracy celebrates the unique virtues of a market wide open to its own initiative.

Thus, after a period of ascent in which it seemed to hold the keys of history, communism revealed in broad daylight the vermin gnawing at its monument to the radiant future of humanity: systematic use of violence, unblinking sacrifice of millions in the pursuit of pharaonic projects, a stunted spiritual life, conformism and methodical manipulation of the masses – all finally leading to the stagnation of society. Today, the plutocracy vaunts its heroic deeds with the same pride and assurance that the communist rulers displayed in their days of glory. Its monuments and symbols are the new skyscrapers of China and Dubai (converted into a 'fun city' for the super-rich); the aeroplanes that serve as flying kingdoms for business magnates; the sumptuous homes of the moneyed princes; the machines and robots producing ever new luxury goods to satisfy needs artificially stoked up by advertising; and the television screens spreading the word of the dominant ideology. And behind this glittering curtain lies the reality that the plutocracy conceals or, failing that, downplays and distorts.

We have seen how the economic potentates try to make governments comply with their strategy. So, governments – and the political forces that support and are supported by them – show a similar attitude to the indiscriminate exploitation of natural resources and runaway environmental degradation: they pursue it with all means at their disposal, the only yardstick being a mode of production geared to the maximization of profit. The danger of an environmental catastrophe now threatens human life. The ecological alarm was sounded very recently, just a few decades ago. For thousands of years, human activity did no more than scratch the earth's crust, as it were, and make insignificant inroads into marine life. Then the industrial revolution brought a qualitative change: without realizing the consequences for the natural environment, and therefore without giving it a second thought, people began to dig and drill, to destroy the forest, and to contaminate the water, air and soil on an ever greater scale. The danger began to be perceived only when quantity turned into quality.

As always, the first to sound the alarm were small minorities of academics; then the 'ballet' got under way. The stakes were enormous, since what was being called into question was nothing less than a philosophy of economic development with no limits other than the capacity of the productive forces and technological constraints on the exploitation of natural resources. The governments of capitalist and communist countries were both deaf to the idea of 'sustainable development' (the latter being even more 'barbaric' in this respect). The scientific community divided into two parties: the first, a majority until quite recently, downplayed the whole issue, denounced 'alarmist' attitudes supposedly based on insufficient, one-sided and misleading evidence, and maintained that global warming and the 'greenhouse effect' were simply an episode in the cycles of nature; the other voice, warning of potential catastrophe, was scarcely heard. In the course of the last decade, however, the relationship between the two has been reversed, as it has become impossible to ignore the danger.

Thus the era of economic globalization is also one in which the gravity of the ecological threat has become widely recognized. And yet – precisely when unmistakeable signs of environmental degradation were beginning to appear, and a group of governments, under pressure from an increasingly concerned public, proposed the very limited measures that led to the Kyoto agreement – the countries mainly responsible for the degradation took the lead in stubbornly resisting the wind of change. The United States, Russia, India and China showed no will to adopt serious measures, fearing that they would be too costly and slow down their own development. And, of course, the great industrial magnates threw their whole weight behind these governments and the effort to mould public opinion. In the United States the George W. Bush administration, an organic alliance of government and plutocratic interests, went so far as to conceal from its own population a number of scientific reports that revealed the growing threat to the environment and called for the adoption of a new policy. Pollution is a global evil, but its effects are particularly dramatic in China and India, the two countries of the great Asian miracle, whose governments have agreed, in the name of economic growth imperatives, to pay a price that seriously compromises the health of their citizens.

Nevertheless, ecological nemesis has become one of the big issues of the day; no one can ignore it any longer. Environmentalists make their warnings heard, while governments of major countries in the world economy sign agreements to limit the 'greenhouse effect'. Yet, although large sections of public opinion are acutely worried about the future of the ailing planet, other sections show a perhaps surprising degree of resigned acceptance as they wait to see whether the predictions are not after all exaggerated. The fact is that, under the guidance and influence of the great economic potentates and their own governments, many people have a mainly passive attitude – partly because, in the rich countries, they fear the cost of an effective strategy of 'sustainable development', while in the poorer countries they think that concern for the environment is a luxury they can ill afford.

It is indeed incredible, from a rational point of view, that governments which have never hesitated in the name of national security to impose the heaviest sacrifices on their peoples in times of international war give proof of such weakness, such uncertainty and such hesitation when it is a question of cooperating against a threat that may one day render the earth uninhabitable. If this means anything, it is that the philosophy of economic development as an end in itself has become a deadly trap, that a gulf is gradually opening up between forces pushing towards destruction of the human habitat and policies capable of containing and combating it, and that, unless there is an energetic reversal of existing trends – and there is no sign of one yet – the future may no longer hold a future at all. For the future of humanity to have a future, we need to relaunch an idea of Progress to govern what currently seems a rudderless world, so that we are capable of responsibly and effectively tackling the problems that confront us.

GIVING THE FUTURE A FUTURE

There was a pervasive optimism about the future in the Enlightenment idea of Progress. Although thinkers were aware of the obstacles in its path, they felt profoundly confident in the light of a Reason that had finally achieved full recognition of its own value and potential to guide human action so long as people wanted, and had learned how, to make good use of it. One thinks here of the trust expressed in Kant's famous essay on the nature and significance of enlightenment. Today – after the final collapse of illusory beliefs in a necessary Progress guaranteed by laws of history – the obstacles seem to come not so much from the legacy of the past as from a future pregnant with threats that men and women are laying up for it in the present. These are now so numerous that we anxiously wonder whether it will be possible to control the hostile forces we let loose every day. For nearly two centuries, the part of humanity located in the earth's most developed areas has ceaselessly intensified its productive forces through science and technology in the belief that this approach brings constant improvements in well-being. Now, however, we face a quite unforeseen situation. Science and technology exceed what would, in previous generations, have been unimaginable even in the boldest works of science fiction; the instruments for the dizzying production of ever more sophisticated goods are reaching extraordinary degrees of perfection; vast regions have broken out of centuries of economic backwardness, while others are emerging from it through their exceptional dynamism; medicine and the greater availability of food resources have made it possible to raise average life expectancy for a large part of humanity. Yet all these huge successes have a reverse side so serious that a sense of insecurity is rapidly spreading in the world. The main question is whether humanity will be able to control the negative energies it continues to release.

To recapitulate: what exactly does this reverse side involve?

First. Science and technology have produced ever more powerful and deadly instruments of mass annihilation, which fill the arsenals not only of the major powers but even of medium-sized ones. The race is on to increase and spread them further, notwithstanding a number of agreements to prevent it. If these agreements have proved to be rather shaky and limited, if they are challenged and disregarded, it is partly because of their underlying assumption that the major, and therefore the strongest, powers should have a kind of monopoly on the legitimate possession of such arsenals. There are even fears that some of the terrorist groups dotted around the world could acquire weapons of mass destruction. By a happy chance that cannot be guaranteed to last, and with the exception of the atom bombs that the Americans dropped on Japan in 1945, the use of weapons capable of unleashing a general or partial holocaust has so far been avoided, thanks more to the terror that each power inspires in the other than to any common wisdom. But the constant accumulation of an ever more deadly and widespread destructive potential presents in itself a terrifying danger, which could result in an explosion if one state or group of states thought that rivals were subjecting it to intolerable threats, or if such weapons fell into the hands of fanatical terrorists convinced that they had nothing to lose and prepared to bring death upon themselves and others.

Second. In today's world, economic development has become a veritable 'golden calf'. The fact that it is guided by the quest for profit is not itself a cause for scandal, since the capacity to make profits is the sign of corporate vitality. What is scandalous is that profits are pursued at any cost and any price by plutocrats who, apart from a small minority, quite unscrupulously manipulate financial dealings to their own exclusive advantage, pay no heed to their social responsibilities, and consider workers' rights as a burden to be reduced as far as possible in the Western countries and ignored in those where workers enjoy no protection (most crudely in post-communist Russia, in still formally communist China and in many other parts of the underdeveloped or developing world). The ideal for the financial and industrial plutocracy is to have the largest possible pool of labour on which it can freely draw for the lowest possible payment. It is certainly a lucrative mechanism, as we can clearly see from the fact that the global income gap between those at the top and those at the bottom has been tending to widen dramatically. No doubt the extension of productive sectors to hitherto excluded parts of the world has the positive effect of tearing large numbers of individuals from the extreme poverty to which they used to be condemned. At the same time, however, the process takes place in such a way as to generate new kinds of separateness, new inequalities, new pockets of marginalization, new poverty – in short, new and extremely grave imbalances. The problem is that, in too great a measure, it is not economic development which is in the service of society but, on the contrary, society which is in the service of the rich and powerful.

The health services, for example, which are ever more efficient thanks to advances in medicine yet also more and more costly, give good protection to the top strata but are tending to become worse for the rest (except in a few countries where adequate welfare institutions are putting up the strongest resistance); cover is denied at an acceptable level to millions of people in the advanced countries, and is totally inaccessible to billions in the poor regions of the world. And it is a scandal that in the strongest country on earth, the United States, where medical research and technology are the most advanced, there is no national health system capable of adequately treating those who do not have a solid bank balance.

Third. The world of democratic states – that is, of governments elected by the people, with a classical division of powers in the liberal mould, recognition of political and civil liberties, and a multi-party system – has never been as extensive as it was at the beginning of the twenty-first century. But, when we look beneath the surface, all too many elements show that much of the earth is still under the rule of authoritarian, even aberrant governments, and that where democracy does exist it is afflicted with serious ills. A number of countries are still not democratic at all. China, the 'miracle' country of our age, offers a historically novel formula combining the dictatorship of a professedly communist oligarchy with a capitalism that does not observe any social responsibility. North Korea is a kind of family monarchy, which also drapes itself in the flag of Marxism-Leninism. And then there are Castro's Cuba, theocratic Iran, Syria, Saudi Arabia and other Islamic states which are a breeding ground for fundamentalism and the international terrorist network inspired by it, and which in Asia and Africa exert a growing influence on the whole spectrum of movements in revolt against the West. The list could be continued. In contrast to all these countries, the democratic West – headed by the United States – puts itself forward as a model and an ideological, political and institutional basis for liberal globalization. In this respect, it is illuminating that the American and British governments, with the real aim of establishing their own rule over a sea of 'black gold', launched the second Iraq war under the banner of exporting democracy. The fact is that Western democracy is a 'worn out' model: it ostensibly bases itself on real popular control over those who exercise power, but this has become increasingly hollow and often borders on outright impotence. The factors hollowing it out are the presence and activity of powers which, in a whole series of cases, completely elude popular control. This is true of the financial and industrial multinationals, which take the main decisions concerning the relocation, reproduction and distribution of resources. It is true of the television news centres, the most important in today's TV age, whose broadcast messages to the world, marked by the 'philosophy' of their owners, mould public opinion in such a way as to make voters into passive consumers in both the economic and the political field. And it is true of those governments – Blair's New Labour and the George W. Bush administration are good examples – which exalt the universal mission of democracy and present themselves as its most zealous guardians in their own countries, but which blithely conduct a secret foreign policy, do not shrink from deliberate deception to achieve their goals, debase the role of the United Nations when they think it an obstacle to their strategy, cover up the use of torture in times of war, and – above all in the United States – drastically curtail civil liberties and suppress basic rights in the name of the war on terror, until society is covered with a surveillance network that brings to mind the spectre of 'Big Brother'.

Fourth. Here we come to the problem that sums up and encompasses all the others. We have to face the fact that, in a world of denser interdependence in the realms of science, technology, economics and communications, there has been a growth of new barriers and mutually separated areas. Evidence of this may be found in the wars conducted by and against terrorism; in the ethnic, religious and cultural conflicts that divide peoples and states; and in the cleavages opened up by extreme inequalities of income, knowledge and power. No international authority seems capable of confronting these barriers and separate areas, or of dealing with them in a manner that could be considered remotely satisfactory. Subordination to the two superpowers during the Cold War ensured, through its very brutality, an international order under the aegis of force. But the idea that the United States, the sole remaining superpower after 1989, might be the pivot of a new international order lasted for only a brief moment. American power did not provide a pivot for the rest of the world to move around: rather, it became a bulwark protecting national interests and those allied with them. And the United Nations, instead of representing the forum for a more incisive 'international democracy', entered a profound crisis in terms of both legitimation and effectiveness. In the scenario that is now taking shape, countries and governments will in effect largely surrender sovereignty to powerful private players in the field of the economy, but will maintain a sovereign foreign policy in subordination to those same players by intervening in disputes and conflicts in this or that area of the globe.

Fifth. While politicians, strategists and academics ask which will be the great powers of the future – whether America will be capable of maintaining its supremacy and Russia will manage to climb back up again after the collapse of the Soviet Union, whether China will rise to the topmost positions and India will grow into a giant in every sense of the word, and whether or how Islamic fundamentalism will be defeated – the world system of states allows the bomb of environmental destruction to accumulate ever greater explosive force.

These are the elements on the reverse side of the coin that make it necessary to develop a new idea of Progress – new in the sense that its contents and purposes have to be brought up to date, though in a line of continuity with the aspirations of those who conceived, championed and disseminated it at the dawn of the modern age. It involves a project for the good society, an ethical disposition to pursue it, the placing of science and technology at the service of communal rather than sectoral interests, and the formation of governments capable of embracing the goals of international cooperation and the cultural and material development of the greatest number.

Almost as soon as one speaks these words, one hears the protest or even mockery of those who dismiss such thoughts as 'facile' and divorced from reality – that is, from the way of the world. In fact, the present way of the world is precisely what necessitates a dramatic turn, one that is not written into some objective movement of history but experienced as a need in relation to the problems besetting humanity, hence as the fruit of a conscious project and a subjective effort of the will.

The wide range of political and social systems that have succeeded one another up to the present day, with the reproduction of the mechanisms of inequality as their guiding principle and internal rule, invariably have three primary characteristics: they give society an internal structure whereby the distribution of the products of human labour especially favours the minorities who hold power; they place human intellectual and physical resources at the service of the exploitation of nature, in order to cover the material needs of the community, without bothering about the 'response' of nature itself; and they reproduce the structure of inequality in the relations between strong and weak countries, so that the former remain at the pinnacle of well-being, while the latter have to endure conditions ranging from mere subsistence to actual poverty, sometimes so extreme that it is impossible to survive. Now, all this is dramatically called into question once the mechanisms of the exploitation of some by others, as well as the exploitation of nature at or beyond the limits of safety, threaten our common survival. This threat manifests itself in the fact that rich people and rich countries refuse to accept that their prosperity should be regulated and contained, while the understandable urge of poor nations to improve their lot asserts itself in unrestrained and irresponsible ways, on the grounds that they can see no reason why they should not follow the path first taken by the advanced countries. Although the alarm bells are ringing loud and clear, governments are unwilling to take the measures that technology itself provides to combat the consequences of incompatible development – that is, to rein in the 'laws' of profit maximization at any cost and a consumerism that accepts no limits; to promote social policies for a more equitable distribution of resources within and between individual countries; and to face up to the urgent task of converting the predatory economy to different ends.

It is this situation, with its knots that need untying, which gives meaning to a new idea of Progress as a possibility, however difficult (because it involves highly complex tasks of world government) and however problematic (because the willingness of countries and governments to address these tasks is today too weak and too constrained by deep contradictions). The prevailing philosophy is evident in questions such as this: 'Yes, it's true, something needs to be done, but how and with what means? Are the costs not too high? And, if others are not on board, why should we take on the burden alone?' The race against time does not leave a wide margin. It is necessary to act swiftly and with a great concentration of forces, but instead the river is allowed to rise without any work on the levees or other measures to contain its fury. Possible Progress could scarcely be more necessary, but we cannot count on history to produce it by virtue of some intrinsic necessity. It is a need that reason suggests to us, but nothing can simply impose it on humanity and force us to act. The impending danger is that, following an oft-repeated method, humanity will wait until it is choking before it takes any remedial action – and by then it may be too late. In our epoch, for absolutely the first time in history, humanity has the perverse power to destroy itself, either with the weapons it has built or with tools that were developed to manipulate the inner workings of the earth itself and are actually poisoning them.

The Enlightenment thinkers developed the modern idea of Progress in full awareness that it was only one possible future for humanity, but they were fundamentally optimistic because they believed in the universality of reason and did not doubt that, if only there was a will, all the means were available to those who intended to use them for the common improvement. Now that the dogmatic illusion of a Progress written in the necessity of history has vanished into thin air, we again find ourselves able to place our hopes only in possible Progress. However, in place of optimism, we have to reckon with a prevailing uncertainty that is difficult to combat because of human pride in the unprecedented power afforded by science and technology and the capacity to accumulate once unimaginable wealth. This sense of insecurity prevents men and women from examining with sufficient clarity the other side of the coin: namely, that all the improper uses of science, technology and material resources have been degrading relations between people and causing imbalances within the natural world.

We should ask ourselves whether we are not actually paving the way for a future without a future. It is a sharp dilemma, and it is high time that we made some unavoidable choices. Not to choose is certainly one choice, the worst of all. But the critical question is whether humanity, after the thousand extraordinary advances that made it so powerful, will also be capable of progress in the development of new social processes – to guide the responsible use of that power in the interests of our planet and all its inhabitants.

A BIBLIOGRAPHICAL NOTE

The following brief bibliography refers to some of the main writings that the author had in mind when he was working on the above reflections.

Andriani, S., *L'ascea della finanza. Risparmio, banche, assicurazione. I nuovi assetti dell'economia mondiale*, Rome: Donzelli, 2006.

Bairoch, Paul, *Victoires et déboires: histoire eéonomique et sociale du monde du 16. siècle à nos jours*, Paris: Gallimard, 1997.

Bury, J. B., *The Idea of Progress*, London: Macmillan, 1920.

Gallino, Luciano, *Globalizzazione e disuguaglianze*, Rome: Laterza, 2003.

Koselleck, Reinhart and Christian Meier, 'Fortschritt', in *Geschichtliche Grundbegriffe: Historisches Lexikon zur Politisch-sozialen Sprache in Deutschland*, vol. 2, pp. 351–423.

Landes, David S., *The Wealth and Poverty of Nations: Why Some Are So Rich and Some So Poor*, London: Little, Brown and Company, 1996.

Nisbet, Robert, *A History of the Idea of Progress*, London: Heinemann, 1980.

Rossi, Paolo, *Naufragi senza spettatore. L'idea del Progresso*, Bologna: Il Mulino, 1995.

Rossi, Pietro, 'Progresso', in *Enciclopedia delle Scienze Sociale*, vol. 3, Rome: Istituto della Enciclopedia Italiana, 1997.

Salvadori, Massimo L., *L'occasione socialista nell'era della globalizzazione*, Rome: Laterza, 2001.

Salvadori, Massimo L., *Le inquietudini dell'uomo omnipotente*, Rome: Laterza, 2003.

Salvadori, Massimo L., *Tramonto di un mito. L'idea del progresso tra Ottocento e Novocento*, Bologna: Il Mulino, 1984.

INDEX